DARE TO DISCOVER...

Who, What, When, Where, and Why

Judith Kay Shroyer Dimmick

Copyright © 2024 by Judith Kay Shroyer Dimmick

ISBN: 978-1-77883-443-1 (Paperback)

All rights reserved. No part of this publication may be reproduced, distributed, or transmitted in any form or by any means, including photocopying, recording, or other electronic or mechanical methods, without the prior written permission of the publisher, except in the case brief quotations embodied in critical reviews and other noncommercial uses permitted by copyright law.

The views expressed in this book are solely those of the author and do not necessarily reflect the views of the publisher, and the publisher hereby disclaims any responsibility for them. Some names and identifying details in this book have been changed to protect the privacy of individuals.

BookSide Press
877-741-8091
www.booksidepress.com
orders@booksidepress.com

Contents

Preface vi
Chapter One: How-tos—Getting Started 1
Chapter Two: A List of Links 4
Chapter Three: A History of My Major Surnames and
Individuals in Them 7
    About Those Antrims 8
    Dunluce Castle 9
    My Many Shroyers 13
    The Girards, a Proud History 17
    Brockways from Britain 20
    "Around the Horn in 1852" (about my great-great-grandfather
    John P. Brockway) 20
Chapter Four: Discovering Heroes That Amaze Me! 23
    Winston Churchill and Family 23
    Jennie Jerome Churchill and Her Family 26
    Descendants of Martin and Jacob Luther 31
    Luthers in America 34
    Three Girard Heroes 38
        Stephen Girard (May 20, 1750–December 25, 1831) 38
        Pierre Louis Gérard (1645–1710) 41
        Count Étienne Maurice Gérard (1773–1852) 43
    More Heroes of the Military 46
        Rear Admiral Richard N. Antrim (December 17, 1907–
        March 8, 1969) 47
        Hospital Corpsman Third Class, US Navy, Wayne Maurice
        Caron (November 2, 1946–November 28, 1968) 48

North American Neighbors 55
   Julien Fortin dit Bellefontaine..*55*
   Charles Thomas Fortin dit Bellefontaine II...........................*58*
   Jacques Timothee Fortin *58*
   Captaine Luc Fortin..*58*
   Jean-Baptiste Fortin *59*
More Recent North American Ancestral Neighbors................60
"The Button" 69
The King's Daughters...70
Artist Ancestors 76
Another Surprising Discovery..82
   Jacques and Antoinette Bernier...*82*
From Great Britain to Connecticut Came the Brockways 93
   Wolston Brockway...*93*
A Challenge to Cope with—My Chayers Who
Were Chailles 98
   Henry III of Castile (1379–1406) *99*
Conclusions and Why Did All of This Matter to Me? 100
About The Author... **107**

To encourage you to study your family history,
the most amazing thing I've done in my life!
With tips on how to do it!

Preface

To best describe my reasons for writing this book and why I hope many will read it, I chose the journalists' old standbys, "who, what, when, where, and why."

Who: *you*, of course! And, yes, *me*. Because of my amazing success, which I owe, first of all, to my grandmother Alda for keeping obituaries, which included Keziah Antrim's, that you'll read more about in this opening segment. *You*—because I want everyone I can reach to study their ancestry and become aware of their own unique history, of which "story" is an important ingredient—one it takes dedication and persistence to discover as many individual stories as possible.

What: "What" can refer to your goal, i.e., how much do you want to include? "What" may mean "What do I do to get started?" or "What can I expect to learn?"—both initially and as time goes by. Of course, the main reason to study genealogy is to document data concerning your ancestors. However, I am amazed at how much I am learning about history, and along with local and world history, the discovery of interesting and scenic places is an added blessing. Something I didn't expect is awareness of connections among surnames and residents. Many even moving long distances together is both fascinating and helpful to the story you are able to create.

When: once you have established your first family tree, the questions regarding when ancestors came to your country, the descendants who were born and who died, etc., will become your concern; and as you add earlier ancestors, you will discover how many people of a certain surname share similar names. Then a comparison of birth and death dates becomes critical.

Where—You might ask where a certain surname was first recorded or where you can find profiles of particular family units. MyHeritage.com won my praise because they send me matches of other clients' profiles that help us each learn something one of us has discovered that's news to the other!

Why: the most common answer to "why?" is probably so you can pass family history on to your children or other family members. Since I've accumulated more than I ever thought possible, a thought came to me just this week. I'll share it with you, hoping if you are blessed with a great deal to share, you'll remember this advice: *write what it would take too long to tell!* However, many more answers are equally important. One I wouldn't have expected to be so important to me is how much I'm learning about history! A simple one is that you may plan to travel somewhere in the world, and now you know which areas could mean most to you. A deeper result is being inspired by what your ancestors were able to accomplish even though life was much harder in earlier times than ours are today.

How: like most people, I would imagine, I started my family tree on paper only. Just by asking my mother and paternal grandmother, I was able to create a family tree with around seventy-five individuals. When my grandma Alda died, however, I discovered she had obituaries of not only her own ancestors but those of her husband, my grandpa Walter. You'll read more about his ancestors in the vignette entitled "About Those Antrims," after the how-to section. It will give you a preview of what's in store for you in the vignettes that follow this opening to *Dare to Discover*. I do hope you'll be inspired to leave a legacy to your descendants that they can leave for future generations.

Chapter One

How-Tos—Getting Started

My *first and most important tip:* Ask all living family—parents, grandparents, aunts, uncles, and cousins—lots of questions about themselves and their ancestors. I can't stress this too much, but here are two vital suggestions:

- *Regarding names*, ask your relative to spell both first and last names. You will be amazed by how many spellings of surnames exist! If they can tell you places of events in the person's life, that will help you narrow down your choice and save you amazing amounts of time! That example reminds me to share this sad fact: without an accurate point of reference on an individual, it may not be possible to document their place in your family's history. Those key items are where they lived, birth dates and/or death dates, and, where possible, siblings and/or names and dates of their children. This comes from the voice of experience, as I have looked at more than a million records on one surname without being successful in providing a family background for a friend. There could be several causes for such a failure; one is that a person changed their name more than once, and therefore, the birth name is unknown. A similar situation could be the relative may have been in a witness protection program. I also learned that birth records were not always required at certain times and places in history, or it may not be clear what country a family came from. Also, language or cultural attitudes may mean facts were withheld or were difficult to understand. I wish I had realized how knowing more details of a person's life would have facilitated my searches. Alerting you here regarding the importance of dates—birth, death, marriage, immigration, military service, etc.—will help you in accessing countless websites that could help you create a better picture of the lives of your ancestors!

For example, I am currently writing profiles of military heroes and have recently discovered how many websites there are about specific battles, as well as ships that were sunk, and specific categories of warriors like the Marauder-Men who flew B-26s in World War II.

This is a good place for a tip you may see repeated in vignettes throughout this book:

Tips: Google is so fantastic, more flexible than I imagined. I have learned to write a complete phrase or sentence with specifics you need, such as "Which king sent the King's Daughters to Canada?" Google answered with countless sources, including this one:

> The King's Daughters. The Filles du roi, or King's Daughters, were some 768 women who arrived in the colony of New France (now Canada) between 1663 and 1673, under the financial sponsorship of King Louis XIV of France.

I found several ancestors who were the King's Daughters, and you will read about some in the next section.

My suggestion to searchers faced with the inability to develop family history on one individual is to concentrate on other family members or surnames. Records may be found for a person closely related that will turn the problem around. Also say, "I'm not going to give up," as new ideas *do* come to mind and available information may surface.

I didn't do a DNA test; they may have existed but hadn't become well-known. What I did was design my own family tree sheets, which helped me greatly when I chose MyHeritage.com as my internet site. Many reasons will be shared throughout this book for how thankful I am to MyHeritage.com. This is an excellent place to add a reference list that I assembled because of my work for WikiTree. Profiles found there can be trusted more completely because they require links that verify where the information came from. The *list of links* that follows is much smaller than the one I rely on, as ideally yours should be when geared to the data and stories you hope to collect.

Chapter Two
A List of Links

Find a Grave, millions of cemetery records (www.findagrave.com): I started with this link as it applies to all types of ancestors we may want to document, and it provides essential data on where else to seek further information we hope to discover.

Billion Graves is a similar site (www.billiongraves): I have accessed this site when Find a Grave didn't provide the sought-after facts.

MyHeritage (www.myheritage.com): If you have chosen this service, as I did, you will find a list of choices that ends with "RESEARCH." You can then select under surname facts in your own family tree or among individuals in the trees of other clients. This is a small example of searches available within www.myheritage.com.

Family Search (www.familysearch.org/en): In addition to services you may choose to pay for, like Ancestry.com or MyHeritage.com, another alternative is Family Search, which is a most important free service. For example, in addition to the very large tree MyHeritage.com enabled me to create, I started with a smaller tree in Family Search with closer relatives for the benefit of my family, and they still e-mail me with new records and information about individuals important to me. You will find countless people throughout history who share the same name as your ancestor. I access the lists in their various searches to select ones that seem to fit what I know about the person.

Geneanet (en.geneanet.org): You can search for your ancestors or even create your family tree there. I find it especially useful for researching

Dare To Discover

European ancestors and appreciate the way trees are presented. In addition to both ascendancy and descendancy charts, clicking "Statistics" reveals surnames associated with the one you have accessed.

Most families include veterans of various wars, from the Revolutionary War through relatively recent wars, so I am continually adding links when I discover sites that may prove helpful.

The National Park Service has done us a great favor by assembling Civil War soldiers in the alphabetical lists under this link: https. This could be a good starting place if all you know about an ancestor is a surname and the fact the individual was in the Civil War. It won't give you all you want, but with the unit he fought in and the complete name, it has helped me a number of times.

There are countless screens on the American Revolution. Digitalhistory.uh.edu covers much more than the American Revolution and is a good place to bone up on the causes, fighting, and consequences of this key event in history.

If you have information on the battles or units your ancestors participated in, you may find pertinent facts on any number of websites. In my case, so many of my ancestors lived in the state of Connecticut that this link was invaluable: https.

Study the pages carefully before you begin your search, keeping in mind that searching through Family Search by your ancestor's name and the war that person served in may get you started. Whatever your situation, prepare yourself for the probability that an extended search could reveal mind-boggling discoveries regarding your family history!

Countless links are available for all the major wars and units of service, so the best advice I can add is to count on Google to find your best possibilities when you enter a search with the best details to identify what you hope to learn. However, if specific honors were received by your relative, these links may help you discover all you want to know. For instance, https://valor.militarytimes.com. Recipients of major awards from the Medal of Honor on down are honored here. There are many; so you must start with the particular conflict, their branch of service, and rank. If you don't have enough of these items, you may still find the individual by searching page by page where you will see the photos of many but at least the names of all who received various honors.

"They also served who now stand forgotten" and *"We also served"* are other sites to check. Fold3.com provides data, but membership is required for more complete service information.

Each of our military services provide lists of websites where you can find data, such as https://www.naval-history.net. Find a Grave and Billion Graves provide detailed data as well as a direction toward sources and, in many cases, photos of the burial sites of veterans. I cannot add all the important links here that help me day by day, but at least, the above examples make you aware of sources that may help you with your collection of family history information!

Chapter Three

A History of My Major Surnames and Individuals in Them

Before you read "About Those Antrims," this poem by Clyde Antrim will explain why I chose the Antrims as a preview of how much can be discovered *if* we are willing to dig:

I never knew I had any kin with the same name as mine,
for my father had told me what had been on his mind.
A long time ago his sister and two brothers had passed away, That I could see was hard for him to say.
After many years I began to wonder—
Who were my grandparents that had the last name the same as mine.
Looking for a needle in a haystack would be easier to find than looking for my grandparents who had the same last name as mine.
After checking records and reading many books,
I found, back in 1635, a man with the last name the same as mine
Came to America to seek freedom and plant seeds of hope.
Throughout history I now do find many men with the last

name the same as mine.

Their deeds throughout history I read with much pride. With friends and neighbors, and God on their side,

They fought the Redcoats and did not run or hide.

Later in battle, their sons would ride, doing battle to set all men free.

These men came from all walks of life, from cities and farms both large and some small, And I can say with much pride, it makes me feel about 10 feet tall.

When I began looking for my family tree, I only had a seed,

But I not only found the tree, but a forest of people with a last name like mine,

And now I can say I'm proud to be an Antrim.

—Clyde Antrim

About Those Antrims

Along with my everlasting gratitude to my grandmother Alda Girard Shroyer, who stirred my interest in Keziah and Adam Shroyer, I must thank MyHeritage.com for a match that provided this proof of Thomas Antrim's arrival in America on June 3, 1635!

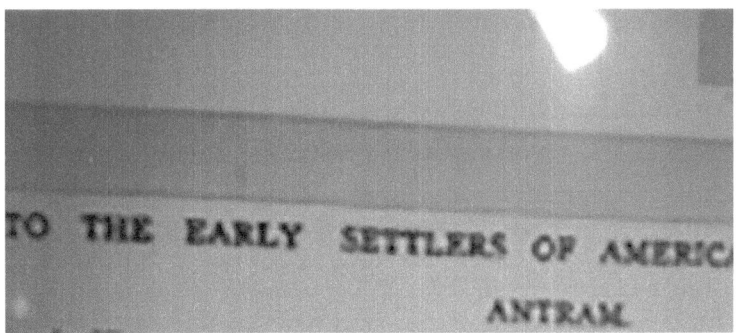

I am also grateful to Clyde Antrim for including this poem I wrote because of the unusual Antrim history in his *Antrim Family Newsletter*:

Dunluce Castle

Dunluce Castle—epitome of mystery to me. It stands atop a rocky cliff in Ireland, Like sightless eyes, its empty windows still seem to search the sea.

Dunluce Castle—home to the great McDonald clan; I wonder, did my ancestors live somewhere nearby? taken to Suffolk, England, these children of long ago,
Ransom for taxes their families could not pay.
Some were taught a trade and given that name—like Butcher, Baker, Carpenter, and Sawyer, But those named Antrim, for the county of their birth, I think McDonalds were who they really were.

—Judy Dimmick

Mary Antrim Roberts was my third great-grandfather's aunt. She wrote an excellent family history. Much of the rest of this vignette is possible because I was lucky enough to receive her story. Yes, that was a piece of luck, but here is my advice to you:

Tip: If you can't find family history written on paper or on the computer but you have heard a family member relate something interesting, ask if you can tape their anecdote and provide a tape recorder, but *don't* trust your memory to remember it until later!

Mary was born in Augusta, Virginia, on October 14, 1794. Her story began with the birth of her father, Godfrey Antrim, in New Jersey in 1753. Around 1776, he married Hannah Haines, the widow of Abram Haines. It is more than remarkable to have what Mary shared about her grandfather, Thomas Antrim! These are her own words: "Being born a gentleman of good position and many accomplishments, he was determined to migrate to the new world concerning such marvelous tales being told to the mother country. A man of good stature, comely visage, enterprising genius, a sound head, vigorous spirit, and generous nature."

I wish Mary would have divulged more about her father and his siblings growing up since one of them was one of my third great-grandfathers! She didn't mince words when she wrote that Thomas Sr. "left all of his children a handsome property, but it soon passed out of their hands through intemperance, extravagance and inattention to business!"

We don't know what happened to every sibling, but we do know that William and Thomas were bachelors and that William died in middle age. Godfrey received money from his father to purchase land in Virginia where he married and had several children, of whom Mary was the eleventh. It is thanks to her sharing of this history that we can understand better how difficult life could be in the 1800s. They moved back and forth between New Jersey and Virginia, finally settling on Backcreek in Frederick County, Virginia. At some point, Godfrey was called away on business, which left his family destitute for a time. The price of bread made it out of reach for Mary at that time. However, a few persons had a small amount of corn. Mary's mother had six yards of woven flannel, and on her way to try to trade it for food, she sat on a log and wept. There, a voice came to her, saying that she would never suffer for bread. That gave her the courage to continue, and she was able to exchange the flannel for six bushels of corn. The next harvest was one of plenty.

Mary lost her father, Godrey, at only four years of age. Her half brother, Abram Haines, came to Virginia to help the family move to Greene County, Tennessee. Here, Mary described her family and wrote how her grandfather, John Painter, born in England, was "bound as an apprentice" at the age of fifteen in order to learn the blacksmith trade. He served under a cruel master and one day received a flogging for eating a slice of bread from the loaf he had been sent to buy. From then on, he worked quietly toward escape so he could seek his fortune in America. He boarded a ship without a cent to his name but later worked out his passage and settled in Virginia. He married Hannah Braddock, whom Mary described as "a very stout, thoroughgoing woman who proved to be a helpmate." Through honest labor and a rigid economy, John acquired property, built a rude cabin and shop, and supported a family of seven children. The sons were named as follows: John, Robert, Thomas, and Isaac; the girls were Jane, Sarah, and Hannah. John became a Quaker but allowed his children to choose for themselves. Mary's mother, Hannah, became a Methodist.

Aiden had moved to Ohio and settled in Miami. He became very religious by about 1820. He said he felt religious "right to the top of his head!" His brother John preceded him to Ohio when he was twenty-one. John became ill and had to return home, where he died three days later. He asked Aiden to take over the land. Aiden worked the land and accumulated more property, eventually adding sixty to seventy acres to a farm of his own. He married Dolly Sharp of Kentucky and joined a church founded by Abel Sargeant of Kentucky. It was known as the Halczon Church.

Aiden was described as "a steady, judicious man, respected by all who knew him." Aiden and Dolly had ten children, but a tragedy kept Aiden from seeing them all raised. When he was around forty, he was returning home from a mill with a sled. A portion of a tree that had "lost its top" fell across the sled and crushed Aiden, killing him. Dolly only survived eighteen months after losing him. She and one son never recovered from the measles. Aiden and Dolly's children who weren't married went to live with a son-in-law, Adam Grove. Aiden's brothers, William and Thomas, came to assist this family, bringing several heads of cattle.

There is much more of Mary's information about family members in my private account of her story, but what I've decided to include from this document is intended to describe how life during the times she wrote about paints a picture of pioneer life in general. When Mary and her family returned to Ohio, I found their journey fascinating. She said they left with "four head of cows," three riding horses, and a four-horse team pulling the wagon filled with household goods, clothing, and two spinning wheels. They traveled sixteen miles the first day, and that night, one of the cows had a calf! They gave the calf to the family in whose home they spent that night.

They continued on up the Clinch Mountains, which were very steep and rocky. She said on several occasions, they had to jack up the wagon to keep it from upsetting. That day's travels took them through Bull's Gap, a Civil War site, onto the Cumberland River and into Kentucky. They passed through Paris, Winchester, and many towns and villages to Maysville before arriving in Clinton County, Ohio.

Obviously, people like Clyde and me are thrilled to have records like these from Mary Antrim Roberts about our early Antrim ancestors in America, but finding out what our surname should have been kept me looking for answers for many years. Only recently, I discovered McDonald of Antrim, born in 1560. He was the father of our James (1585–1632) and Thomas (his birth is listed as in 1575)! Having earlier learned that many McDonalds were massacred in Scotland by the Campbells and those who survived ran off into the countryside, it seems logical to me that the McDonalds who got away might have come to Ireland since the McDonalds are on record as residents of Dunluce Castle. Maybe sometime, I'll find further proof of this discovery that pleased me so much, but until then, I'll thank God that I've learned so much about my Antrims!

Another answer to my earlier question "Why?" I already mentioned my hope of encouraging others to discover their family histories, to which I can add what I imagine is a common desire of most readers—to have a foundation upon which their descendants can continue to build. Now I must add what I consider the most important reason—to know ourselves, which is why I chose the title "Who Am I?" I saw examples on the BYU channel's program *The Generations Project* of people gaining courage to face painful losses, doubts about what careers they should follow, and many other challenges. And just yesterday, I cried over something I discovered. A highly regarded person in my life, though not a relative, became one of the moderators of the General Assembly of the United Presbyterian Church. I wanted to find a photo and facts about this achievement to share with others.

I was unable to find more than one photo that didn't do him justice and was stunned that I checked so many sources but found nothing like what I wanted. That may be the conclusion of that particular desire of mine, but what I'm learning through my dedication to staying hopeful concerning the results of my decades-long quest is that our efforts may lead to further knowledge we could not have predicted, and if we stay connected to sources of trustworthy information, we will end up with the best conclusion possible.

My Many Shroyers

Since my great-great-grandfather, Adam Shroyer, married Keziah Antrim, that is the next history I chose to cover. Adam's father was George Washington Shroyer, who was born in 1792 and died in 1858. He was buried in the Greenwood/Harvey Cemetery near Urbana,

Illinois. An article I found in volume 7, issue 3 of the *Champaign County Genealogical Society Quarterly* (December 1985) indicated that the cemetery was in terrible condition at that time. Vandals had destroyed many of the monuments and some that were carried away. Luckily, the DAR transcribed the cemetery in 1961. It had first been surveyed in 1870.

Adam's mother was Margaret Bennet, who was born in 1788 in Pennsylvania. I have not been able to find more about her, but luckily at the time of her husband's death, she placed an ad I ran across asking their children to contact her regarding the legal aspects of their father's death. That was a lucky break that helped me put my Shroyer ancestors' story together!

Tip: What I learned in the next part of this section is *don't* ignore any results from a search because you don't expect to find something there. I don't remember how my search was worded, but the notice for heirs of George Washington Shroyer to contact their mother was the door to finding that George Washington Shroyer's father was Matthias Shroyer, a soldier in the Revolutionary War.

Luckily, I located records on Mathias showing that he was receiving a pension in 1835 at the age of eighty-two following his service in the Revolutionary War! Thankfully, on Memorial Day 2019, I found his name on the list of soldiers that were part of the German Regiment in the Continental Line. This just reflects the history of the formation of the troops that would defend the territory that is now our United States.

Early in the year 1776, anticipating the possibility of hostilities with England, the Continental Congress decided to raise an army from the thirteen colonies, each colony to furnish a quota of officers and men based upon the size of the population and the ability to procure arms and supplies. This was the genesis of the Continental army, as distinguished from the local colonial militia forces.

In addition to the regular colonial units, Congress authorized the establishment of a number of additional regiments. One of these was the German Battalion composed of officers and men selected from among the German settlers of Pennsylvania and Maryland. Accordingly, in the spring of 1776, the Continental Congress, in pursuance of this objective, passed several resolutions as follows:

- "Resolved that one Battalion of Germans be raised for the Service of the United Colonies" and
- "Resolved that four companies of Germans be raised in Pennsylvania and four companies in Maryland to compose said regiment."

I wanted to find specific actions that included this fifth great-grandfather. The timings of these battles are likely good representations as, of course, I wasn't able to find individual coverage of his participation but feel extremely lucky to have found this document on Fold3.com. In August 1777, the reorganized German Battalion had its first action in the night raid on Staten Island. After initial success, the American forces were driven into retreat. Despite heavy fighting, the German Battalion escaped with only minor losses. After the British landed at Elk River, the scene of the war was shifted to the area between Wilmington and Philadelphia.

The German Battalion was guarding the crossing of Brandywine Creek at Chadd's Ford at the beginning of the Battle of Brandywine on September 11, 1777. The seasoned riflemen forced a strong contingent of Hessians under General von Knyphausen to abandon the initial attack. But then tactical mistakes and rivalry on the part of some American commanders and a superb strategy of the British and Hessian forces led to a disastrous defeat. The German Battalion suffered most severely. The extent and severity of these losses are indicated by the fact, as stated in Heitman's Historical Register of the Officers of the Continental Army, that the manpower of the German Battalion had been reduced from the original nine companies to two companies which spent the winter of 1777–1778 at Valley Forge, plus a detachment of Maryland Germans who were in winter quarters with General Smallwood.

The commander under whom Matthias served was Charles Baltzell, who was born in Alsace on October 15, 1737. He took part in the defense of the frontier against the Indians, and after the defeat of General Braddock, he was appointed first lieutenant in the German Battalion. He was wounded at the Battle of Germantown, on October 4, 1777; however, he recovered and continued in the service with the battalion until January 1, 1781, when the battalion was retired. Lists were included in this document in an effort to recreate a composite of the soldiers who made up the German Regiments. My ancestor's name appears in one of the many spellings of our surname, "Schreier," in the Muster Roll of Capt. George P. Keeport's Company of the First German Battalion, Continental Troops!

After the British landed at Elk River, the scene of the war was shifted to the area between Wilmington and Philadelphia. The German Battalion was guarding the crossing of Brandywine Creek at Chadd's Ford at the beginning of the Battle of Brandywine on September 11, 1777. The seasoned riflemen forced a strong contingent of Hessians under General von Knyphausen to abandon the initial attack. But then tactical mistakes and rivalry on the part of some American commanders and a superb strategy of the British and Hessian forces led to a disastrous defeat.

The German Battalion suffered most severely. The extent and severity of these losses are indicated by the fact, as stated in Heitman's Historical Register of the Officers of the Continental Army, that the manpower of the German Battalion had been reduced from the original nine companies to two companies which spent the winter of 1777–1778 at Valley Forge, plus a detachment of Maryland Germans who were in winter quarters with General Smallwood.

Another aspect of Matthias Shroyer's life was that he developed the muskets used in the American Revolution, which added to his success and fame, as I see evidence of gun production in the lives of his descendants. I was also anxious to find all I could about his ancestors. I haven't found stories about their lives in Germany and the

United States but am grateful for the names and dates of the lives of many. Matthias's father was Hans George Schreier, who was born in Kirchenbuch, Friedelsheim, Rheinland-Pfalz, Germany, on July 22, 1725, and died in Baltimore, Maryland, in 1722. His parents were Christian and Maria Kroff Schreyer. We know that Christian was also born in Friedelsheim, Palatinate, Bavaria, Germany, in 1658. Maria was born in 1690 and died in 1738.

The Girards, a Proud History

Since my grandmother Alda's maiden name was Girard, the following was a major question that stirred my interest in family history. As I lived in several big cities, I got to wondering why so many have streets or avenues named Girard. Eventually, I learned of the amazing life of Stephen Girard, at one time known as "America's First Tycoon."

Later, when I worked in a Trust Department of a bank, his story gave me a perfect illustration of what investing a fortune wisely can do. Stephen left no living children, but his Trust Fund is still providing an excellent education at Girard College nearly two hundred years after his death.

By never abandoning my search to find out if any of his ancestors are mine, I found the connection to the brave Pierre Girard who left France in 1669 for New France, which we now know as Canada. That Pierre who was born in 1645 was my sixth great-grandfather, and I couldn't have been happier than when I learned he was Stephen Girard's grandfather!

I wish you discoveries like that in your family tree. I almost said "I wish you luck," but instead of *luck*, keep these words in mind: *research* and *study*. Then there's another word I wrote a little joke about *curiosity*. My joke is set in heaven where I decided that I had heard God was giving out curiosity, and judging by my life, I must have gotten in line twice! Another Girard discovery you'll read about is Etienne Maurice Gerard, such a great French general that his name is etched in the Arch

A History of My Major Surnames and Individuals in Them

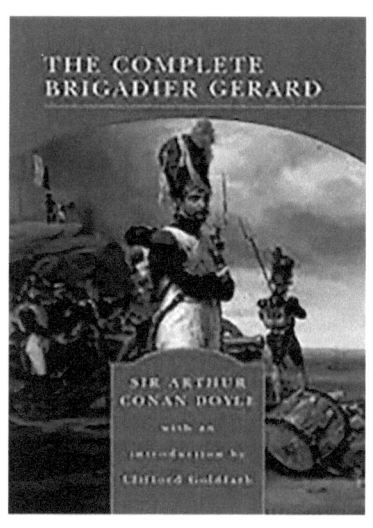

De Triomphe. I recently discovered that Arthur Conan Doyle of *Sherlock Holmes* fame wrote books based on Gerard's adventures!

Tip: After depending on matches that provide me with the important basics: names, dates, places, and relationships, I have found Google searches often provide interesting episodes in the lives of many of my ancestors. That, in itself, is a "tip," but another is that Google photos sometimes offer valuable information through a choice "Visit Site." You may not only see representations of the person searched for but often connected in some way to the surname.

Another important tip: To help you avoid pitfalls and achieve your goals regarding your ancestry, think early on about all you want to achieve. Some people just want chronological lists of people within their closest surnames. Others, like me, want to learn what their lives were like and to go as far back in history as possible. I also chose to include all surnames connected by marriage.

Looking for Girards' way back in history taught me many things, but this tip will help if you run across French surnames in your search:

Two tips in one: Set up computer folders for records on surnames you expect to find. You may find variations of spellings, but your folder can simply be the one your family bears. With French names, I learned what *dit* and *dites* indicate. When you see *dit* or *dite*, it indicates that when the first settlers came to Canada from France, it was a custom to add a *dit* nickname to the surname. The English translation of *dit* is "said." They may have wanted to distinguish their family from others by taking a *dit* name to describe the locale to which they had relocated. The use of a *dit* name might also be the result of a casual adoption to honor the family that raised them. Another reason was to show the name of the place in France where the family originated. This custom ended around 1900, when people began using only one name, either the *dit* nickname or their original surname.

I can't stress how important this tip is except to explain why in detail! First, I must tell you how this came about… I had amassed a long list of ancestors in several surnames, and in the case of Girards, a few on my list go back to the 1400s. I thought, "Wow! If I can get that far back, I'd like to discover who the first Girards were… One day, I thought, "Why not see what Wikipedia has on this surname?" I was thrilled to find a section on "The House of Girard" on the internet and soon learned it was related to a man with the title Count Girard I of Paris. I can't share the whole story here, but two facts will help you understand the significance of this discovery. First, because Girard married Rotrude, the granddaughter of Charles Martel, it put their children in line for becoming the leaders of many parts of Europe. This was my understanding thus far of the naming history over roughly 1,200 years ago. As I struggled to cope with the lack of a surname and the repetition of given names, I wondered why they didn't carry the surname Girard.

It is very important to remember that it wasn't until William the Conqueror, who conquered Britain three hundred years after Count Girard lived, issued an edict that his subjects must choose a surname. I read that some countries under his rule didn't get far with that until the 1600s. However, Ireland got it done in that same century!

The second discovery I made about those early "Girards" was that the parents of Count Girard I had two sons, one named Girard spelled with an *i*, the other son with an *e*. Of course, if you are already "into" genealogy, you have probably found that many surnames had several spellings over time. My maiden name, Shroyer, is a good example, with at least half a dozen other spellings that I am aware of and one that has a story I enjoy, which is that Schreier, in Germany at one time, meant "town crier"!

A History of My Major Surnames and Individuals in Them

Brockways from Britain

My great-grandfather Philip Girard chose Hattie Brockway as his bride, and my grandmother Alda first introduced me to her grandfather John Brockway's life, and later a cousin shared the amazing story of her great-grandfather's life. He, John Pockman Brockway, his father, Chauncey, and his brother traveled "Around the Horn" to the Gold Rush in California. I wrote a poem that includes many of their experiences during that trip. Before I share more about that fantastic journey, it's important to tell of their ancestors. If not for the first Wolston Brockway in America, I might not have discovered Wolston Brockways existed back in the eleventh century in England! I can only tell you how I got there—it was through hard, determined work! I suppose John Pockman and his close family's adventure going to the Gold Rush by traveling "Around the Horn" convinced me that amazing episodes in the lives of our ancestors can be found!

"Around the Horn in 1852"
(about my great-great-grandfather John P. Brockway)

Six months at sea, Oh glory be! And his Pa was sick as sick could be.
This letter survives from my great-great-grandfather who sailed 'round the Horn to California.
He recorded their progress on many a day along with the hardships that came their way.
Not only seasickness but smallpox, too, Affecting the passengers and the crew.

But nothing was worse than the following worry—The Captain was stricken with apoplexy.
This happened in August, over three months away from the start of their voyage,

The Fourth of May, In the year of our Lord, Eighteen Fifty-two— I'll return to that day and share more with you.

They lay in some stream, which is all he did say, until they were towed on the Eighth of May.

Past Sandy Hook they hoisted their sails, faced choppy waters but no strong gales,

Yet they crossed the Equator the 19th of June and "hoved into sight" by the light of the moon.

A convict island, rough, rocky and small, this Brazilian landmark, exceedingly tall,

May have looked to them like a giant church steeple, and no doubt amazed these travel-worn people.

He described July Fourth as "a most splendid day"—an American vessel came sailing their way.

It being Sunday, they waited one day to celebrate in a most festive way.

The flag was hoisted and gunshots went up.

There were speeches and toasts before they could sup.

John wrote in detail of how they fared—

Boiled ham and rice pudding among what they shared.

At the Isle of St. Catherine they stopped July Nine, and he wrote that the Bay was exceedingly fine.

How long they stayed I really don't know, But John wrote about the crops they could grow.

Among the foods these Portuguese grew were oranges, lemons, and pineapples, too.

On July Nineteenth they sailed toward the Horn and encountered snow one frosty morn!

August Ninth brought a wind extremely strong; It raged against them a full day long.

But had it continued for "24" more, it could have driven the North Star ashore.

Later in August, I so hate to say, a great many porpoises came their way.

They harpooned one and served it up, which may have been hard for me to sup.

On September Eleventh they crossed The Equator, and not long after they ran low on water.

He didn't write much for many a day except about storms that came their way.

At last in October they caught sight of land. "The land of gold" was the phrase he penned.

It was on the Nineteenth when the fog cleared away, so they could behold San Francisco Bay.

He described what they saw as a splendid sight, many vessels around them both day and night.

By this time he wrote that no one was ill, and they all looked forward to eating their fill.

The pilot told them that business was good; He also shared the prices of food

—

But butter and sugar could seldom be bought, two pork and potatoes were more to be sought.

On October Twenty-first Brockway wrote to a friend that their trip at last had come to an end.

"We are now fixing to go ashore," John gave as the reason he couldn't share more.

But we are so blessed that this letter survives to give us more insight on these ancestors' lives.

—Judy Dimmick

CHAPTER FOUR

Discovering Heroes That Amaze Me!

*A*s I got deeper and deeper into researching the histories of various ancestors, I was fortunate enough to find several instances of relationships that occurred because of marriages down through the centuries. This one meant so much to me because I grew to admire Winston Churchill greatly through books he wrote and being aware of World War II history (which may have been more meaningful to me because I was born at the time of the Battle of Britain)!

Winston Churchill and Family

Winston Churchill was the most surprising discovery that occurred, finding someone I could never have imagined was connected to me by ancestry! I had already read Their Finest Hour and begun to find and read all I could about Winston Churchill by the time I lived in Seattle. However, something happened there that contributed to my declaration that he is the greatest hero of the twentieth century, at least for me. I met a woman who was the pastor of a community church near me and eventually asked her to meet me for lunch downtown. In our conversation that day, we discovered we were born on the same day in the same year—September 8, 1940, during the Battle of Britain. However, I was the lucky one, born in Wray, a small town in Eastern Colorado, while she was born in a subway that served as a bomb shelter in London!

On the night I started this chapter, I rewatched the movie *The Battle of Britain*, which zeroed in on the early days of that terrible bombardment of Great Britain by the Nazis. In addition to the great actors Sir Laurence Olivier, Christopher Plummer, and Michael Caine, I felt an angel visited me when one of the scenes was filmed in a subway shelter just like my friend described, reminding me of her and how utterly devastating World War II was for the English and so much of the world. Churchill's words below are probably the most memorable speech of that war or any other:

> We shall go on to the end. We shall fight in France. We shall fight on the seas and oceans. We shall fight with growing confidence and growing strength in the air. We shall defend our Island, whatever the cost may be. We shall fight on the beaches. We shall fight on the landing grounds. We shall fight in the fields and in the streets. We shall fight in the hills; we shall never surrender, and even if, which I do not for a moment believe, this Island or a large part of it were subjugated and starving, then our Empire beyond the seas, armed and guarded by the British Fleet, would carry on the struggle, until, in God's good time, the New World, with all its power and might, steps forth to the rescue and the liberation of the old.

It would be impossible to include all of Winston Churchill's achievements, but I'm mentioning a few so you will grasp how astounding it was to learn this great hero and I share ancestors! His third great-grandmother was the sister of my fourth great-aunt. Many will know of his exciting experience as a young man in the Boer War...being captured, escaping, and reporting to newspapers in England during a time when newspapers were the main source of news.

During World War I, he served as Lord of the Admiralty and in the Royal Scots Fusiliers on the Western Front. In 1917, he returned to government under David Lloyd George as the minister of Munitions, secretary of state for War, secretary of state for Air, and then secretary of state for the Colonies. After two years out of Parliament, he served as chancellor of the Exchequer. And even though he served as prime minister twice, words can't describe adequately how important his leadership was. He received so many awards during his life that I have chosen two of great importance: Knight of the Garter by Queen Elizabeth was one of his favorites, but receiving the Nobel Peace Prize for Literature was the honor that impressed me the most.

Churchill came to the United States twice and had a close relationship with President Franklin Roosevelt and later President Harry Truman. I saw his granddaughter Celia Sandys on PBS in a special named *Chasing*

Churchill and was thrilled to see her in the Brooklyn house where Winston's mother was born. That 1895 trip was when Winston fell in love with the United States. I love these words from Mark Twain: "By his father he is English, by his mother he is American—to my mind the blend which makes the perfect man."

Jennie Jerome Churchill and Her Family

LADY RANDOLPH CHURCHILL

Winston's mother was considered one of the most beautiful women in the Victorian world, but she had many talents that contributed to her fame. It all started with this: Jennie's father was a stockbroker and businessman known as the "King of Wall Street" in New York City. It is said he made and lost several millions. At one point, he gave his wife, Clarissa, one million dollars to provide their three daughters a classic education. During the Victorian age, Paris was the penultimate place for a higher education. As part of their learning experience, Jennie's mother took her daughters to parties in both London and Paris so they could mingle with the British aristocracy or at least make new and important connections.

In 1873, at a sailing regatta on the Isle of Wight, Jennie met Lord Randolph Churchill, and just three days later, they became engaged. I've read that Lord Randolph told a friend soon after meeting Jennie that she would be his future wife! Lord Randolph and Jennie were married in 1874. It was at Blenheim Palace that their first son, Winston, was born on November 30, 1874.

The author Robert Lewis Taylor described Blenheim as a "gigantic stone pile, not dissimilar in size and shape to Buckingham Castle." There were 320 rooms, with gardens, parks, ponds, streams, forests, and grassy hillocks, for a total of 2,700 acres! This grand palace was a gift to Winston's ancestor, the famed duke of Marlborough, who fought many battles but is best known for the Battle of Blenheim on the banks of the Danube on August 13, 1704. That explains why the fabulous gift of thanks from Queen Anne was named Blenheim. During the short time Jennie lived in Blenheim Palace, she must have been impressed with the tremendous treasures that surrounded her. However, her remarks on how her father-in-law ran the palace reveal how his influence had a positive effect on her. He was so against idleness that he designated several hours during the day for self-improvement. Jennie said she practiced piano, read, and painted to such an extent that she began to imagine herself back at school!

Winston's brother, John, was born in 1880 during the time Randolph served his father when he was Viceroy of Ireland. Jennie was immensely popular during their stay in Ireland, not only because of her radiant beauty but also her outstanding wit and sense of humor. Eventually, the family moved to the couple's house near Marble Arch in London where their house was the first in London to have electricity. Jennie's days were spent doing charity work, shopping, and entertaining; so it was not surprising that she sent Winston to a boarding school. However, he wrote that his mother made a spectacular impression on him. He added that he loved her dearly but at a distance. It was obvious his parents left much of his care to his nannies, governesses, and nurses. One nanny described Winston as the naughtiest boy in the world. Fortunately, his last nurse, Mrs. Everest, got on well with him and remained a positive influence in his life.

Lord Randolph Churchill did not live a long life; born in 1849, he died in 1895. After his death, Jennie pursued literary efforts, editing a magazine for a short period of time and writing several books and plays. Her articles "Short Talks on Big Subjects" were published in *Pearson's Magazine*, and she became known for quotes such as "There is no such thing as a moral dress. It's the people who are moral or immoral." Jennie was also known for her patriotism. During the Boer War, she managed to purchase *The Maine*, a two-hundred-bed hospital ship. Jennie was often a subject of the tabloid papers because of numerous lovers and admirers, including King Edward VII, after Randolph's death. She married twice more; her second was to a captain in the Scots Guards ended in divorce, and a third husband was a British civil servant, that marriage lasting until her death.

Tip: When I learned of my connection to Winston Churchill, I wondered, "How many other members of this family have led fabulous lives that I should study?" I've already alluded to Jennie's father, Leonard Jerome, of whom I'll share more next, and will also include a few facts about her mother, Clarissa Hall.

Leonard Jerome was described by his grandson Winston as "very fierce!" Although one of ten children who grew up on a farm in upstate New York, tending chickens and livestock, as an adult, he had a knack for making money. His career as a stockbroker earned him the informal title "the King of Wall Street." It is said that hostesses loved having him at social events because he was not only handsome but also a charming civic leader like rumors regarding Jennie during her lifetime, publicity about adulteries involving her father ran rampant, the most notable being Jenny Lind.

In addition to his unrivaled success as a businessman, Jerome was appointed American Consul in Trieste by President Millard Fillmore. He served in that capacity for only eighteen months, but that was long enough for Clarissa to become fascinated with European society.

Thoroughbred horses were also among Jerome's successes. He owned Jerome Park Racetrack, home to the first Belmont Stakes.

Just like in modern times, the financial markets had their ups and downs during Jerome's career; and by 1880, both his health and wealth had taken a downturn. By 1888, he retired completely from business, devoting his flagging energy to looking after his horses. Because of his failing health, Leonard Jerome left America for the last time in his life in December of 1889 and died on March 3, 1891. More important than all the achievements mentioned above, it was believed that his greatest achievement was his grandson Winston's inheritance of traits such as astuteness, zeal, personal motivation, and wittiness.

    Regarding Clarissa, Leonard fell in love with her after meeting her at a ball. It struck me how mother and daughter's lives were changed dramatically by one social event! She, too, was an heiress to what was described as a "small fortune." Still, I read that it was five years before they were married in April of 1849. Clarissa (who wanted to be known by Clara) and her sister were daughters of Ambrose Hall, a landowner. During the years Clara spent in Paris, she became so accustomed to the extravagant balls and parties of the era of Napoleon III that when the Jeromes returned to New York, Leonard purchased a large lot on the corner of Madison Avenue and Twenty-Sixth so he could keep his promise to her that he would build her a palace!

    I wrote most of these histories and saved them separately as they came to me. Now I wish I had recorded what I learned when. Since I did not, they are assembled more in the order of how amazing they were to me at the time. I hope what may be gained is learning a great deal of history because of the lives of these ancestors.

It was much later that I learned of my connection to this historic family, for lo and behold, Martin Luther and his brother Jacob are also part of my heritage!

Descendants of Martin and Jacob Luther

I was afraid to include the information until I was able to see the connection through Martin's son Johannes. Before that, I had verified these earlier ancestors:

- The earliest: Weigang Luder, whose name came to me without dates. His son: Haine von Luder (1431–1509)—bauer (farmer or peasant) of Möhra, Thüringen, Deutschland, and his wife, Margaret Ziegler. Their son: Hans Luder (May 29, 1459–May 28, 1530) and his wife, Margareta Lindemann (1459–1531), also of Thüringen, Deutschland. Their sons: *Martin Luther* (1483–February 18, 1546) and *Jacob Luther* (1490–1571). Martin's son Johannes carries us to my great-grandmother and her descendants, including me!
- *Johannes Luther* (1517–1584)—Mansfeld, Mansfeld-Südharz, Sachsen-Anhalt, Germany; death: Drohndorf, Aschersleben, Salzlandkreis, Sachsen-Anhalt, Germany
- Father of Johan Luther (1537–1561)—Mansfeld Germany to Stapleford Tawney, Essex, England
- Father of Johann Jacob Luther (July 6, 1561–December 4, 1621)—Stapleford Tawney, Essex, England; Katherine Coleman, London, England
- Father of John Samuel Luther (December 11, 1597–March 25, 1644)—Great Cranford, Dorset, England; murdered on a ship in Delaware Bay, Massachusetts, United States
- Father of Rev. Samuel Luther (October 25, 1636–December 20, 1716)—Bristol, Massachusetts, United States

- Father of Samuel Luther II or Jr. (October 25, 1663–July 23, 1714)—Bristol, Massachusetts, United States
- Father of James Luther (March 8, 1693–December 15, 1777)—Bristol, Massachusetts, United States
- Father of Phebe Buffington (August 26, 1731–before 1772)—Swansea, Bristol, Massachusetts
- Mother of Preserved Buffington (December 20, 1759–July 23, 1843)—Swansea, Bristol, Massachusetts
- Father of *Content Buffington Brockway* (April 3, 1786–Mar 15, 1857)—Dover, New York, Shodack, New York (Married *Jesse Brockway*)
- Mother of Chauncey Porter Brockway (June 24, 1807–January 4, 1890)—Shodack, New York; Geary, Kansas
- Father of John Plockman Brockway (March 1, 1833–June 18, 1921)—Rensselaer, New York; Vining, Kansas
- Father of Hattie Jane Girard (November 16, 1874–October 16, 1964)

—Vining, Kansas; Amarillo, Texas

Tip: I included this verification in case anyone doubts my claim regarding being related to Martin Luther. It is distant, that's true; but if anything could surprise me more than my Churchill discovery, this is it!

I imagine most readers know of Martin Luther's life and importance to Christianity, especially Protestants. Thus, I will include lesser-known facts after stating all these titles that apply to him in addition to his role in forming the Protestant Reformation. He was also a German professor of theology, composer, hymnologist, priest, and monk! During this research, I learned for the first time that the day Luther posted the Ninety-Five Theses for an academic debate on indulgences on the door of the castle church at Wittenberg in 1517 was Halloween!

Dare To Discover

News of his controversial action spread quickly. In a debate with the theologian Johan Eck in 1519, Luther stated even more radical theological positions, resulting in Eck gaining a papal decree against him. After refusing to recant during his meeting with the Imperial Diet at Worms, Luther was taken for safety to the castle of Wartburg where he began his translation of the Bible into German. In 1522, he returned to Wittenburg to continue the significant writing that continued throughout his long life. Among his most important works were the *Great Catechism* and the *Small Catechism*, his collection of sermons and hymns.

Discovering Heroes That Amaze Me!

The Luther Family

It is wonderful that a picture with his family exists, a most important part of the life that began with Katharina von Bora in 1525. She was a nun who left her convent, as other nuns were doing, to marry a monk. They had six children of their own, but the household also included one of Katharine's relatives, and after 1529, six of Luther's sister's children. Their household was not only busy because of these children; at times, there were up to twenty-five children and student boarders under their roof. Martin's famous Table Talk also took place at mealtimes. The students were often at their table and asking questions into the late hours of the night.

Luthers in America

Captain John Luther (1597–1645): The first of the family to come to America came to Boston from Germany by way of Dorset, England, in 1635. He was one of the original proprietors or founders of Taunton, where ninety acres of land were assigned to him. Nine years later, we find him a master of a sailing ship belonging to a company of Boston merchants and chartered to open trade with a colony of Dutch and Swedes on faraway Delaware Bay. Sailing into the Delaware Bay for the first time, his ship was boarded by a band of Indians for the supposed purpose of trading. Instead, they had hatchets hidden under their blankets and murdered the captain and two of his men.

Rev. Samuel Luther (1636–1716): He married Mary Able in 1662, the same year he applied for buying land in Rehoboth (a name said to mean "roomy place" in biblical times). Samuel was ordained to the ministry at the Baptist Church of Swansea in 1683, where he continued until his death in 1716. The most amazing fact I discovered about Samuel is that he was uneducated to the point of not being able to write his name, so documents were signed with his mark. His character was such, however, that he held positions as selectman and representative to the General Court. So well respected was he that the current congregations meet in "the Elder Luther's Church."

Elizabeth Luther Weeks (1626–1687) and Sir Francis Weeks (1618–1687): Francis Weeks was born in Broadsword, Devonshire, England, in 1618. He may have arrived in Salem, Massachusetts, in 1635 on one of two ships, the *Providence* or the *Expedition*, which left England in November of 1635. We know his whereabouts the following year, for when John Smith was banished, he asked to be allowed to take a boy, Francis Weeks, with him to Providence, Rhode Island. The General Court of Massachusetts had ordered on September 3, 1635, "that John Smith be sent within these six weeks out of this jurisdiction, for diverse dangerous opinions." It was in 1636 that *Roger Williams*, John Smith, and four others came to Providence and made the first settlement there. History confirms that *Francis Weeks was one of the four on the boat in this drawing. Roger Williams (c. 1603–1683) is best remembered for founding the state of Rhode Island and advocating the separation of church and state in Colonial America.*

Discovering Heroes That Amaze Me!

In 1641, Weeks was in New Amsterdam; in 1648 in Gravesend (now part of Brooklyn, New York); in Hempstead, New York, in 1657; and later at Oyster Bay, Long Island, New York. On June 14, 1663, he was one of those chosen to map and lay out Oyster Bay. In 1667–1668, he was constable and overseer. In 1668–1669, surveyor. And in 1669, he was a fence viewer. It would be interesting to know what that entailed!

I chose to include Elizabeth Luther and Sir Francis Weeks because I found their experiences ideal to help us understand the challenges and circumstances our early settlers faced. Elizabeth had already faced a devastating situation when her father, Captain John Luther, was murdered by that band of Indians who supposedly boarded his ship for the purpose of trading. Instead, they had hatchets hidden under their blankets and murdered the captain and two of his men in Delaware Bay. The life of Francis, who had been associated with the likes of John Smith and Roger Williams, obviously prepared him for success in positions he held in New York.

Tip: You may experience controversies, as I did here, on whether Francis Weeks's wife was Elizabeth Luther. This is how I handle such situations (where legal records, like a marriage license, are not available).

I look at many records and tally how many agree with the decision. In this case, I looked at most records of both Francis and Elizabeth and at *all records of their many children!* The total who agreed that Elizabeth Luther was the wife of Sir Francis Weeks was forty-six, against only two with a differing choice.

When I found the Weeks had nine children, I searched for an image of Elizabeth to honor her as well as countless others who bore and raised long lists of children in the early years in North America. I am also amazed by the courage it took to leave their homelands across the seas. Add to that the grief of losing children who died in infancy and childhood. Not finding an illustration of Elizabeth, I chose the above image to give us a glimpse of a mother's life centuries ago.

Discovering Heroes That Amaze Me!

Three Girard Heroes

Stephen Girard (May 20, 1750–December 25, 1831)

  This was the Girard that answered my questions about the streets named Girard. However, I don't remember how I learned of this amazing Girard, but at some point, I began to wonder if he was connected in any way to my line of Girards. I can now understand that until I learned of his grandfather, Pierre Louis Girard, I didn't have the background to connect Stephen with Pierre's son of the same name! I am now as stunned to discover the man called "America's First Tycoon" was a distant cousin as when I learned Winston Churchill is a distant ancestor. In some ways, it is even more amazing that Stephen Girard became so successful, as he was the oldest in a family of nine children and had no formal schooling. He was taught by his parents because there was no system of public education in France at that time.

At just fourteen, Stephen first went to sea, but only ten years later, he was captain of his own ship, involved in trade with the West Indies. In time, he developed a fleet that traveled the world and managed this business with such efficiency that when he sold the ships, he was able to purchase the first bank of the United States, which he renamed the Bank of Stephen Girard! This Philadelphia Bank provided credit to the US government and during the War of 1812 when US credit was at a low ebb. Girard's 95 percent investment in war loans enabled the US to win that war!

Not only was Stephen Girard an outstanding businessman and manager, but I found his private life admirable too. He had no children, no doubt due to the illness of his wife, Mary Lun, the daughter of a Philadelphia shipbuilder who was born in 1758. Stephen and Mary owned and operated a store in Mount Holly Township, New Jersey, before moving to Philadelphia. There they sold a variety of items to locals and American revolutionaries.

When they had been married eight years, she became emotionally unstable and suffered uncontrolled rage which caused her to be committed to the Pennsylvania Hospital for the insane in 1785. A baby girl was born to her there who only survived five months. Mary was there for twenty-five years, until her death in 1815, even though she was given the best care available then.

Unfortunately, the feelings of famous people who suffered such sadness were not often recorded in the nineteenth century, but another of Stephen Girard's claims to fame does reveal to me his reaction to the above losses in his life. He created and endowed what he named the Girard College for Fatherless Boys. It is still going strong under the name "Girard College." When I worked in a trust department of a bank, the fact that Girard College has survived for over 160 years was an excellent example of how endowments well invested can benefit others for countless years.

Discovering Heroes That Amaze Me!

Girard College, Philadelphia, 1886

Another example of Girard's concern for his fellow Philadelphians occurred in 1793 when an outbreak of yellow fever struck the city. While many other wealthy citizens left the city, Girard stayed and not only converted a mansion outside the city limits into a hospital and recruited fellow citizens to nurse the victims but also cared for patients himself. He led efforts in the outbreak of 1797–1798 to help his city survive another health disaster. Nothing could make me happier about deciding to research my ancestors than discovering how just this one ancestor lived his life, benefiting so many during his lifetime and continuing to bless the youth who are able to attend Girard College because of his generosity and concern.

Tip: I don't know what you'll discover about your ancestors, but having discovered all the above I'm sharing with you, I feel your descendants will be glad for any history you can assemble for them. I also imagine you will not only learn about family but will arrive at a greater understanding of yourself and what influences your family history has contributed to your life.

So this tip is don't miss out on this enriching experience!

Pierre Louis Gérard (1645–1710)

It was exciting to receive the history of Pierre Louis Girard because with the record of his parents, Etienne and Marguerite Gibouleau Girard, I was able to verify that Pierre was my sixth great-grandfather! Matches from MyHeritage.com on Pierre also provided an answer to a question I had long been curious about—was the amazing Stephen Girard related to my branch of Girards? When I checked on Pierre's children, I found his son, also named Pierre Louis, was the father of Stephen Girard, which makes him a cousin!

This Pierre was raised in the town of Les-Sables-d'Olonne, Poitou, France. A long time ago, the citizens of Olonne fished for cod and whales, so Pierre often gazed at a group of rocks in the Atlantic, watching the movements of the tides. Did the possibilities of travel across the ocean and awareness of nearby citizens leaving France for a new world of opportunity, then called New France, enter his mind? I'm sure my hopes and dreams would have gotten the best of me, so I feel sure the answer is "Yes!"

At nearby La Rochelle, a great number of ships came and went. It's quite possible that Pierre found work at La Rochelle during his youth, as in 1669, he was there with the title of a mariner. On August 11, 1669, he married Suzanne Lavoie, the widow of a cobbler, Jean Tesson, in Quebec. Suzanne had returned to La Rochelle as a childless widow, and her history shines a light on how Pierre Girard ended up in Quebec. Philippe Birot, a merchant, witnessed the signatures of Suzanne and

Pierre on their marriage contract and noted that the contracting parties were about to embark for Canada. And Pierre is listed as a passenger on *Saint-Pierre de Hambourg*.

Upon arriving in Quebec in the summer of 1669, Suzanne Lavoie would certainly have introduced her new husband to her father, Pierre Lavoie, in the suburb of Saint-Augustin. In New France, a newcomer had to work for three years in the service of a responsible employer before gaining the rights and privileges of a colonist, and Suzanne's father no doubt helped Pierre achieve that status. I have not learned a great deal about the lives of Pierre and Suzanne except that they were living at Saint-Augustin in 1677. Their first child was born at Beauport a few years earlier. The Jesuit Guillaume Mathieu had the baptism recorded in Quebec.

There is no evidence of a concession of land to Pierre Girard; but the census of 1681 reports Pierre and Suzanne living in Maur where they owned one gun, five head of cattle, and had twelve arpents (a unit of similar to an acre) under cultivation. Pierre had also become master of a barge named *Le Saneud*, that did coastal trading on the St. Lawrence River. One record that points to his success as a businessman came from Sieur Daveau, who ceded the right to the eau-de-vie and tobacco of poor quality brought from the islands. A tax of two sols only per pound of tobacco, and not of five sols, was ordered to be paid by Girard. Girard complained to the authorities about taxes on the eau-de-vie, saying that money was being extorted from him because he sold his alcoholic beverage at a lower price than that imported from France. An official ordered that Girard need only pay two-thirds of the rate France paid per ton.

By 1688, Pierre Girard was a widower and married Elisabeth Lequin, who had been one of the King's Daughters and twice a widow. Although she and Pierre did not have any children, her son, Pierre Leveille, married Girard's daughter Jeanne in April 1700. Pierre is the only widower I've read about who married a widow who came to Canada as one of the King's Daughters.

Count Étienne Maurice Gérard (1773–1852)

When I read the meaning of *Girard* is "people of the well-tempered spear," I was glad I found Etienne Maurice, whose life seems to fit that definition. In accessing the above picture of him, I realized Wikipedia entitled it "prime minister of France." During his fascinating life, he was also a French general and marshal of France. He was a son of Jean Gérard (1739–1801), a royal bailiff, and an auditor of the royal prevostura of Damvillers and Marville in Northern France.

Étienne participated in all the campaigns of the First Empire and ascended to all the degrees of the military in France. As marshal of the empire, he was wounded in Austerlitz while brilliantly charging as head of his squadrons against the Russian Imperial Guard. He was promoted to brigadier general on November 13, 1806, after showing great daring at the Battle of Halle. At Jena, Etienne charged the Prussian cavalry and took a large number of prisoners. He also served as chief of staff of the IX Corps of the Army at the head of the Saxon Cavalry. Gerard contributed significantly to the French victory, and in 1809, Napoleon I made him baron of the empire.

Gérard became count of the empire by imperial decree in January 1813. On the second day of the Battle of Leipzig, he received a serious wound to his head, which forced him to cede the command. However, he managed to reestablish himself in time to take part in the Six-Day Campaign in 1814. Gérard was a part of too many victories to mention, but his achievements were so outstanding that Louis XVIII made him a knight of the Royal and Military Order of Saint Louis as a token of his esteem, and he was appointed inspector general of the Fifth Military Division. In 1815, Gérard became inspector general of infantry in Alsace. Upon the return of Napoleon, Etienne received command of the Army of the Moselle, which became the IV Corps. It was elevated to the dignity of Pari de France on June 2, 1815. Delivering the new imperial insignia to his troops, he said, "Soldiers, here are the new eagles the Emperor entrusts to your valor; those of Austerlitz bring fifteen years of victories; to you the task of giving new proofs of courage: the enemy is in front of you!"

Following the success of his troops in the Battle of Ligny, he was heading for Wavre when gunfire was heard from the Soignes Forest. The corps commanders were reunited with the council: Gérard argued that, following the general principles of war, they head for the cannons. One, "Grouchy" opposed the idea, based on different orders from the emperor. This movement could perhaps have changed the result of the Battle of Waterloo. By the end of the day, Gerard was wounded for the fifth time, a Blücher avant-garde ball hit him in the chest while attacking the village of Bierges at the head of the infantry. He, nevertheless, wanted to remain close to the troops and was transported beyond the Loire.

After the capitulation of Paris, Gérard was one of the generals who negotiated with the new government on behalf of the army. After that, he retired and went to Brussels, where he married Louise Rose Aimé de Timbrune-hiembronne de Valence, second daughter of General de Thiembronne. The couple had three children: Georges Cyrus Gérard (1818–1841), diplomat and embassy secretary in Constantinople; Louis Maurice Fortuné Gérard (1819–1880), cavalry colonel and officer of the Legion of Honor, who died without getting married. (Thru a relationship with Sylvie Perruche, from whom the poet Rosemonde Gérard was born) Nicole Etiennette Félicité Gérard (1822–1845), who married Laurent Arnulf Olivier Desmier, Count d'Archiac, without a descendant. They returned to France in 1817 and settled in the castle of Villers-Saint-Paul (Oise).

Girard continued to serve France in various elected positions. During the July Revolution, he actively supported the cause of the duke of Orléans and was appointed minister of War by the Provisional Municipal Commission in charge of administering the capital in the face of the lack of civil and military authorities. Louis Philippe elevated the title to marshal of France in August 1830. When he left the government officially for health reasons after being deemed too interventionist with regard to Belgium, Belgium offered him his last great military victory. Marshal Gérard was called to command the Army of the North. After thirteen days, he forced the dutch to evacuate their positions in Belgium except for the citadel of Antwerp. On his return to Belgium on November 15, 1832, he laid siege to Antwerp, which capitulated on December 23. This victory earned him a sword of honor as a token of gratitude from Belgium.

On February 11, 1833, he was appointed a peer of France, and on July 18, 1834, Gérard was called as prime minister while still holding the ministry of War. He was appointed grand chancellor of the Legion of Honor on July 28, 1835. He abandoned his function in December

1838 to replace Marshal Mouton as commander in chief of the National Guard. His last great honor was to be appointed senator of the Second Empire on January 26, 1852. Gerard died a few months later. His body, with those of his wife and three children, is buried in a crypt of the church of Nogent-sur-Oise.

I was surprised that his fame was such that Arthur Conan Doyle even wrote books about him. Looking for other Gerards named Etienne and Maurice, I found this Etienne Maurice Gérard! For a long time, I was concerned about the two spellings of Girard until I found the parents of Girard Count I of Paris had two sons. One is spelled *Girard*, and the other *Gerard*. It looks to me, after searching the records of many, that difference in spelling probably occurred because of where they served. Lots of challenges occur because surnames didn't become common until William the Conqueror's decree that Europeans choose a surname for their families and their descendants.

More Heroes of the Military

Since I became a WikiTree genealogist in my late '70s, my appreciation has grown for how many lives have been involved in preserving the freedom of my own country as well as the whole free world! Some gave significant years of their lives, others the ultimate sacrifice; but the entire magnificence of their combined service overwhelms me as I add my small contribution to WikiTree's goal of creating One Human Tree so that family and friends of these heroes can access what we have gathered without charge! Here are a few of the heroes I can trace to my ancestry, some close relatives, some more distant, but all so worthy of appreciation in my humble book.

Rear Admiral Richard N. Antrim (December 17, 1907–March 8, 1969)

As an executive officer of the *Destroyer Pope*, which participated in the desperate struggle to defend the Philippines and Netherland East Indies, the *Pope* was sunk by aircraft bombs. Although injured, Lieutenant Antrim led the survivors for three days while lost at sea. The enemy picked them up and took them to a prisoner of war facility at Makassar, Celebes. In April 1942, when a fellow officer was being viciously beaten and close to death, Antrim bravely stepped forward and offered to take the rest of the punishment, stunning the Japanese guards, inspiring the Allied prisoners, and creating among the enemy a newfound respect for their American captives. For his "conspicuous gallantry and intrepidity" on this occasion, Antrim was awarded the Medal of Honor. He also found a way to communicate the location of the camp. After liberation in 1945, he received specialized training and continued in strategic duties, becoming the head of the Naval Amphibious Warfare Section. Upon retirement, he was awarded the rank of rear admiral.

Discovering Heroes That Amaze Me!

Hospital Corpsman Third Class, US Navy, Wayne Maurice Caron (November 2, 1946–November 28, 1968)

During combat operations against enemy forces in Quang Nam Province in the Republic of Vietnam on July 28, 1968, while on a sweep through an open rice field, Hospital Corpsman Third Class Caron's unit started receiving enemy small-arms fire. Upon seeing two marine casualties, he immediately ran forward to render first aid but found them dead. The platoon was then taken under intense small-arms and automatic-weapons fire, sustaining additional casualties. As he moved to aid his wounded comrades, Caron was hit in the arm by enemy fire. Though knocked to the ground, he regained his feet and continued to the injured marines. He rendered medical assistance to the first marine he reached, who was grievously wounded. He undoubtedly was instrumental in saving the man's life. He then ran toward the second wounded marine but was again hit by enemy fire, yet he crawled the remaining distance and provided medical aid for this severely wounded man. He started making his way to yet another injured comrade when again struck by enemy small-arms fire. Courageously and with unbelievable determination, Caron continued his attempt to reach the third marine; however, he was killed by an enemy rocket round. It's hard to imagine bravery greater than this! Wayne Maurice Caron received the Medal of Honor posthumously.

Wilfred Mapon Chaille of the Fifth Light Horse Regiment in World War I: I decided to include "Pat" Chaille because many hours of researching people with the surname Chaille convinced me that, like Girards, we are all related to some extent. I am a descendant of an American family which should have continued with the surname Chaille but was misunderstood and changed to Chayer in the United States. I was surprised to find Chailles in Australia, but it was touching to learn that in 1920 Pat Chaille was buried at Wadi Manahan in the Jordan Valley after he was killed in action when encountered by German snipers near the River Jordan in what was then Palestine. In 1920, his body was exhumed and now is interred at the Jerusalem War Cemetery in Israel, memorialized with this touching inscription that quoted his parents, James and Charlotte Chaille of Esk, Queensland: "A happy, cheerful soul was our boy Pat, beloved by all who knew him."

Discovering Heroes That Amaze Me!

The discovery of this Civil War hero caused me to discover the amazing array of Griswolds in the family of John Griswold: Captain John Griswold, who was born on April 24, 1837, in Old Lyme, Connecticut, and died on September 17, 1862, at the age of twenty-five, during the Battle of Antitetum, Sharpsburg, Maryland. He captured my heart more than any other hero I profiled for WikiTree. I don't know why, but it may have been because it was my first encounter with the Civil War and also because of the loss of the tremendous potential of such a talented young man. September 17, 1862, was considered the "deadliest day" in the Battle of Antitetum. As if that wasn't bad enough, it still remains the bloodiest day in American history with 23,000 casualties among the 120,000 fighting men. General Ambrose Burnside commanded the Union forces on the Rohrbach Bridge where the Confederate soldiers were on high ground on the other side, opposing the Union soldiers' efforts to cross the bridge. The Connecticut Eleventh was first to try to cross the bridge under Colonel Henry Kingsbury, who was quickly struck by four bullets and soon died. Captain Griswold waded into the creek, leading the men in A Company. However, before reaching the other side, he, too, was shot down. John was a graduate of Yale and Captain of Volunteers in the Civil War. John Griswold is buried in the Griswold Cemetery, Lyme, Connecticut. This memorial note was posted in 2009 by Glenn Harman:

> Captain Griswold, You died a brave man with your face to the enemy. Your dedication and courage will never be forgotten. RIP.
>
> Babette Griswold was a schoolmate of mine, and I recently wished I could talk with her about this hero of the Civil War, a young man I thought might be closely related to her; but by the time I discovered this history, she herself had died.

I wanted to know more about how the Griswolds were connected with my Brockways, so I pursued records of other Griswolds and put this list together:

1. Alda Mary Shroyer was my grandmother; Hattie Jane Brockway Girard was her mother.
2. John Pockman Brockway was the father of Hattie Jane Girard.
3. Chauncey Porter Brockway was his father.
4. Jesse Brockway was the father of Chauncey Porter Brockway; Nathaniel Brockway was his father.
5. Dorcas Brockway was the mother of Nathaniel Brockway.
6. Eunice Wheadon was the mother of Dorcas Brockway. Jane Swaine was her mother.

7. Ann (Hannah Griswold) Bronson, nee Westover, was the mother of Jane Swaine.
8. Margaret Winslow Griswold of Killingworth was her mother.

I just recently noticed that Luke M. Griswold and Captain John Griswold were both born in 1837. I wondered how they were related. The only way to find out was to look for Luke's father's name. I was happy to find I had already entered Luke into WikiTree, and that profile gave me his father's name—Zopher. That unusual given name presented a bigger challenge than anticipated—I couldn't find him in our American records; but fortunately, when I did a search on Google, a site turned up that gave me his place of birth, which was Digby, Digby, Nova Scotia. I recommended earlier that a person should decide at the beginning of researching their family what the scope of their search should include. This is a good example of what I decided *and* of how at this point I limited the extent of my search for Brockways to those with some connection to the United States. So when it turned out Luke Griswold's father, Zopher, wasn't connected with the Brockways I have studied, I decided I could better use my time on Griswolds with connection to people and places the two families have in common.

Luke M. Griswold (1837–1892) was buried in the Oak Grove Cemetery, Springfield, Massachusetts: He was a Medal of Honor recipient because of an important event in our history. Luke was described as an ordinary seaman in the Military Times Hall of Valor. He was serving in the US Navy, aboard the USS *Rhode Island*. That ship was engaged in saving the lives of the officers and crew of the USS *Monitor* near Cape Hatteras, North Carolina. After rescuing several of the men, Seaman Griswold became separated in a heavy gale with other members of the cutter that had set out from the Rhode Island and spent many hours in the small boat at the mercy of the weather and high seas until finally picked up by a schooner fifty miles east of Cape Hatteras. That is not the end of the story, however. The following link covers the work of US representative Richard E. Neal, who wanted heroes of the Civil War to be honored fully.

Rep. Richard E. Neal visited the grave site of Medal of Honor recipient Luke M. Griswold and found only a marker to note Griswold's grave, but on April 30, 2013, Seaman Luke M. Griswold's moment of recognition arrived. The gravestone was arranged by J. Donald Morfe of Baltimore, Maryland, an Army veteran and retired executive for BlueCross BlueShield of Maryland. Thanks also to the Congressional Medal of Honor Foundation, the gravestone was installed in time for Richard Neal to visit the grave on that Memorial Day when Neal stated, "It is only fitting that…this son of Springfield receives the proper recognition for what he did in the Civil War."

Since 1999, Morfe has helped to install memorials for 220 Medal of Honor recipients from Washington, DC, to Alaska and Hawaii. Along with other volunteers, Morfe photographs graves, decorates them with American flags, and when necessary coaxes the government or private groups to buy new gravestones. Considering that the Medal of Honor is the nation's highest wartime honor, Morfe never expected to find so many recipients lacking decent memorials.

As a Civil War veteran, however, Griswold had no Social Security number. He died in 1892, four decades before the first numbers were issued. He also lacked any traceable next of kin—a requirement for getting a government-funded gravestone. After months of wrangling, Morfe gave up and convinced the Congressional Medal of Honor Foundation to pay the roughly $500 fee for the new gravestone. Little is known about Griswold's life after the war. He died in 1882; his wife later died in the city's poorhouse. "He was lost to history," Morfe said. That ended on April 30, when Oak Grove agreed to install the Medal of Honor grave marker free of charge. Last week, Morfe visited the cemetery to photograph the new gravestone. "It's wonderful," he said. "There's something to honor him now."

Another John Griswold (April 24, 1837–September 18, 1862) was the son of Elizabeth Griswold (born Perkins). It was sad to learn he only lived to age forty-eight, since, as a Yale graduate, he became a lawyer, justice of the peace, probate judge, and member of the legislature. The colonel married Ellen Elizabeth Perkins on November 14, 1820.

The colonel's father was renowned Roger Griswold (May 21, 1762– October 25, 1812). The fact he only lived to be fifty reminds me of how life spans have changed remarkably in the last three or more centuries! His accomplishments in such a short lifetime are amazing… He was a US congressman, in Twenty-Fifth Connecticut, a governor, and born the grandson of Connecticut governor *Matthew Griswold*. Roger graduated from Yale College in 1780, studied law, was admitted to the bar in 1783, and commenced to practice law in Norwich, Connecticut. In 1795, he was elected as a Federalist to the Fourth Congress and the next five succeeding Congresses, serving until 1805. He then served as a judge on the Supreme Court of Connecticut, in 1807, and then as a lieutenant governor of Connecticut. In 1811, he was elected as a Federalist governor of Connecticut, serving until his death at age fifty. Among his top concerns were issues that resulted from the War of 1812.

Matthew Griswold's history amazed me. His reputation as a fair and hardworking lawyer won him the appointment of king's attorney for New London County. The king's attorney represented the interests of England and her colonies in court. That Griswold held this position for over thirty years stands as a testimony to both his ability as a lawyer and his fair-mindedness.

Still, I was surprised to read that later he was a strong supporter of the colonists' cause during the American Revolution. He served on many committees that oversaw troop movements, military appointments, provisions, and defense; he especially focused on defending American ships and the Connecticut shoreline. According to family legend, Griswold twice evaded British soldiers as they searched for him, an important target, in his own home. In 1788, as a delegate from Lyme, he became the president of Connecticut's convention to ratify the new United States Constitution.

Later in 1788, Ursula Griswold died, and Matthew Griswold retired from public life. He continued to manage his family estate, Black Hall, until his death on April 28, 1799. He is interred at <u>Duck</u>, Old Lyme, New London County, Connecticut.

North American Neighbors

Canada: Our neighbor to the north brought me the most surprises in regard to surnames closely associated with my family. Here are some of the most amazing:

Julien Fortin dit Bellefontaine

It speaks volumes to be able to include the Ancient Coat of Arms that represents the importance of Julien Fortin, who was a tenth-generation ancestor of mine and an early Frenchman who left France for New France! Born in 1620 or 1621 in France, he played a significant role in the success of what we now recognize as Canada. One of his descendants, Melanie Fortin, married Moisi Girard; and their sixth child, Charles, was my great-grandfather's father! Moisi was born in Baie-Saint-Paul, the town I fell in love with through connections to ancestors MyHeritage.com revealed to me. Now I wish I had visited that part of Quebec before I got "too old," since Montreal and St. Ignatz, I've learned, have great significance in the history of my French ancestors! More about Marc-Aurele Fortin will appear with other fabulous ancestors/artists in this book.

One reason the discovery of Julien and Genvieve Fortin is so extraordinary to me is learning how important one family could be to a new country! In this case, it was New France, which we now know as Canada! My direct ancestor Julien Fortin was the first of seven Fortin men to arrive in New France. His mother, Marie Lavie (or La Vye), died when he was only seven years old. Julien's father, also named Julien, was a butcher. His maternal grandfather, Gervais Lavie, was the owner of the famous Cheval-Blanc Inn. There Julien heard stories told by Seigneur Giffard about life in New France. Dr. Robert Giffard was also the proprietor of the Seigneurie of Beauport in New France. Giffard returned to France in 1650 to recruit people in Perche to become a part of New France. Julien, then twenty-nine, departed from Dieppe in Normandy and spent three months at sea before arriving in Quebec in the summer of 1650 because of the influence of Dr. Giffard.

Julien Fortin

It is important to know that Julien was born in Saint-Cosme-en-Vairais, Pays de la Loire, France. As I continue to learn about Julien and his sons, like Charles Thomas Fortin, who was a captain of the militia in Canada, I realize how important the bravery of the first pioneers from France was to the success of Canada. Upon arrival in New France, Julien lost no time purchasing waterfront property (December 26, 1650), right in front of St. Anne de Beaupre. After selling that property, he became part owner of two seigneuries, Beaupre and the Ile d'Orleans.

The dictionary describes *seigneury* as "a landed estate held in Canada by feudal tenure until 1854." Julien also acquired Lot No. 149 in the territory known as La Petite Rivière de Saint Francois in Charlevoix County. By 1661, during the Iroquois Ravages, Julien testified in court regarding the sacking of two nearby farms and the murder of six people, one of whom was his son-in-law, Louis Guimond. Julien was already at ease when he arrived in New France and remained so throughout his life. Michel Langlois wrote in his *Dictionnaire Biographique des Ancêtres Québécois* that Julien was able to lend money but was never a usurer. On the contrary, his generosity was legendary.

The exact date of Julien's death is not known, but it was sometime between 1699 and 1700. Genevieve lived at the home of her son Charles after Julien's death and was buried on November 5, 1709. I have included this couple because their lives are such an excellent example of life as pioneers along what is now referred to as the "Fortin Coast" and because of the amazing lives of their descendants in New France and later Canada.

Charles Thomas Fortin dit Bellefontaine II

This couple's oldest son became a lieutenant of the militia. He was born in St. Anne de Bupre, Quebec, Canada, on November 17, 1656, and died June 22, 1735, in L'Islet-sur-Mer, Québec, Canada. Charles and his wife, Saint/Xainte (Cloutier) Fortin, had one daughter, Elizabeth, who was born in 1695 but died in 1733. Her husband, Francois Guimond, lived to the ripe old age of eighty-two!

Jacques Timothee Fortin

He was born on July 25, 1742, and died on November 3, 1709, both in Cap-Saint-Ignace, Montmagny, Québec, Canada. Although I have not found more about this fourth child's military career, he was the father of Clement Luc, who lived from 1797 to 1871.

Captaine Luc Fortin

He was born on June 16, 1797, and died on January 4, 1871. Captain Fortin was the grandson of Jacques Timothee Fortin (born in 1742) and Marie Louise Bernier. At the age of twenty, around 1817, he and his parents, Clement Luc and Marie Madeleine Gaudreau Fortin, moved to Henryville. Luc became quite wealthy but was always generous to the less fortunate. Because of his loyalty to the Crown of England, Luc Fortin was selected to be a captain of the local militia. He was so proud of this honor that he wanted it to be attached to his name.

Luc was the last man one might think would become suspected of disloyalty to the English authorities, but that is what happened during the disturbances of 1837 when several citizens of the parish of Henryville joined the ranks of the "Sons of Liberty" Militia. Captain Luc Fortin, being of good judgment, remained completely out of the revolutionary activities that marked this turbulent period. He was against his compatriots attacking a power impossible to conquer due to the lack of organization, weapons, and resources. He especially blamed Louis-Joseph Papineau, who was leading the French-Canadian rebels toward a disaster. In 1837, when the battles of St. Denis and St. Charles failed, Papineau fled because of the price on his head. He wanted to cross the border into the United States, and at Henryville on the road to Vermont, Captain Luc Fortin gave him food and had his helper harness a horse and take Papineau to the border, so Papineau evaded his pursuers and arrived in Vermont. A man named Etienne Poulin, who drank too much, revealed that Fortin had helped Papineau to escape. The military arrested Fortin, but he escaped in the night to a former presbytery where he had hidden out earlier. The above situation calmed down, and Captain Luc Fortin died on his farm on January 4, 1871, after a busy life. He was seventy-four years old and mourned deeply by friends and neighbors.

Jean-Baptiste Fortin

He was a captain in the militia. He was a son of Charles Fortin, born in 1701; he died on February 8, 1770, at age sixty-eight in Cap-Saint-Ignace, Montmagny, Quebec, Canada. I searched for more about his life and found a record of Jean-Baptiste's marriage to Francoise Belanger on October 25, 1723, in L'Islet, Canada, New France. The couple had at least seven children. However, I was disappointed that I was unable to find any records of his service as a captain of the militia. This will have to remain on my list of mysteries. As Paul Harvey, an American radio personality, was known to say, I still hope to discover "the rest of the story."

More Recent North American Ancestral Neighbors

These are histories of more recent ancestors who came to the United States from Quebec, Canada. I turned to a book on my own shelf, the *Girard Genealogy*, which was compiled by Alpha Fay Girard, a cousin of my grandmother Alda Girard Shroyer who went by "Fay." I met his twin brother, Alphonse, who worked with one of my Heindel cousins in Colorado Springs (just a reminder of what a small world it is!). Another brother was revered by all who knew him. I'm placing a photo and portions of Monsignor Armand Girard's obituary here because his life was so outstanding and no doubt known to many ancestors in this section of "North American Neighbors."

Armand was one of eight children born to Leon and Blanche (Desilet) Girard on April 26, 1921, in Aurora, Kansas. He was ordained on June 10, 1945, in Sacred Heart Cathedral, Salina, and was a licentiate in canon law. His first assignment was at Sacred Heart Cathedral in 1947. Four years later, he was made prochancellor of the diocese and held that position until 1954 when he was assigned pastor of Saints Peter and Paul Parish in Clay Center where he supervised the building of a new parish hall and enlargement of the church. In 1959, he was appointed as the first pastor of St. Mary Queen of the Universe in Salina and was instrumental in enlarging the St. Mary's grade school and the building of the interparochial high school while also serving as vicar-general.

Monsignor Girard visited Rome and attended some sessions of the Second Vatican Council. From 1967 until his retirement in 1995, he served several churches and held other distinguished roles such as vicar general, serving on the Diocesan Board of Consultors, membership on the priest's Senate, the Diocesan Pastoral Council, and the Consultative Board of Marymount College in Salina. He died on January 5, 2005; and his Mass of Christian Burial was held on January 10, 2005, at the St. Mary Queen of the Universe Catholic Church in Salina, Kansas.

The monsignor's uncle was my great-grandfather Philip Charles Girard. He and his siblings were the children of Charles and Philomene Girard, and I wondered if they were among the followers of Father Chiniquy who led groups of Catholics from Quebec to Illinois. Since their son, Philip Charles, was born on September 10, 1861, in Montreal, Canada, and was a young man when he accompanied his parents and siblings to Illinois, it seems clear they weren't part of the groups that traveled with Father Chiniquy. Since I haven't been able to find lists of all the many people who followed Father Chiniquy, I may never know for sure who all of them were.

In order to understand more about what inspired so many people to emigrate from Canada, I started by reading this brief paragraph from Alpha Fay Girard's genealogy:

> It is unknown as to why this generation left Canada. They could have been part of the great influx of Canadian immigrants that entered the USA between 1871 and 1901. Taxation, debts, failing commercial and industrial enterprise and unemployment led to over two million Canadians with shattered dreams to seek economic refuge in the United States.

Discovering Heroes That Amaze Me!

The Saint Joseph Area History, a cousin gave me this remarkable treasure that provided most of the material in the rest of this vignette, except for the information on Kankakee, Illinois.

My Google search gave me January 4, 1817, as the date Kankakee, Illinois, was founded. I found a city directory for 1873 and wrote down all the names in the alphabetical list who are also among surnames in my tree.

- Narcisse Belanger, a laborer; and Frank Belanger, a painter
- Mrs. V. M. Langlois, a dressmaker
- Leon Bergeron and Isaac Bergeron, harness makers
- Felix Papineau, a mason
- Joseph Benoit, a carpenter
- Rousseau, only the surname is given
- J. Gautier, owned a butcher shop
- Roy, A., Homer and Alfred
- Heny Regnier

In a faded book of prominent people in Kankakee, I could barely make out any of the names. Though portraits of couples were quite clear, I finally found one more man bearing the surname of one of Quebec's most successful families, Timothy Fortin. The only other fact about him I could barely make out is that he was born in Henryville, Quebec, where Girards and other ancestors lived at one time. Finding only the above names assures me that most of my closer ancestors went on together after the terrible floods that ruined crops and disrupted the lives of those who decided to move on to Kansas. This book would never end if I tried to find all the other Canadians who came to the United States, so keep in mind that Kankakee, Illinois, and Cloud and Clay Counties in Kansas were chosen by me as representatives of this period in our history, and how thrilled I am to learn how my father's French ancestors arrived here and how much it has contributed to my understanding of myself and my country's history.

Cloud County, Kansas, Canadian Settlers in St. Joseph, in particular: I want to give credit and thank individuals who provided the fascinating information in the November 1995 *St. Joseph Area History*. They indicated it was published in the *Advocate*, a Kankakee, Illinois, newspaper: Shirley Coupal, John Cyr, Vernon Forgue, Mabel Odette, and Norma Meier. I won't be able to include everyone mentioned but will cover as many as possible with interesting stories.

There's a faded picture in the above book called an old-fashioned mobile home because it had wooden coverings rather than canvas. I wish I could show it, but words will have to do. After the Civil War, advertisements appeared to lure settlers in "sider" states with glowing statements urging them to sell out and come to the fertile fields of Kansas…send for free maps and general information.

Among my ancestors, *Laurent Charbonneau* married my third great-aunt *Melanise Girard* at Iberville, Québec, Canada, in 1856. They left Montreal in 1863 and lived in Illinois until settling in Clyde (St. Joseph) in 1879, where he died in 1911. My records show one of their daughters was Felia Charbonneau Tremblay, born in St. Joe in 1870. Melanise's mother was *Melanie Fortin Girard*. Seeing the names

Fortin, Tremblay, and Girard together points out how ancestors from one area, at least mine, often traveled together, since all these families were together in Baie-Saint-Paul, which I discovered when I was so amazed that three ancestors were the founders of Baie-Saint-Paul.

The conditions the early settlers experienced will apply to many of the ancestors I will mention. One of the most difficult was living in dugouts or soddies. Soddies were built above ground from sod, not an ideal way to live. They are small and sometimes invaded by snakes and other pests! In order to provide for the family and their animals, wells were dug by hand, and water was fetched in buckets. By 1880, possessions of the French coming from Kankakee arrived on one of two railroads. The earlier English settlers seemed amused by the French pioneers, mostly because of the difference in language and volume of their conversations. However, these newcomers were good farmers and brought new hard wheat from Russia called "Turkey Red." All inhabitants in this part of Kansas had to endure drought and, in 1874, grasshoppers which attacked all green vegetation. So many crops were lost that those who could not survive moved on, some back to Illinois.

After the Civil War, the government offered homesteads to Union Army veterans; and more than one hundred thousand took advantage of that, greatly expanding the population in the region. With this growth, many were settling on farms, but some were forming the town of St. Joseph, often called simply "St. Joe." A few years later, another small town, Como, started up. It was never more than a few houses and a general store that later sold gasoline once cars came onto the scene. One of the owners years later was Hector Girard, a cousin of my grandmother. One of my goals is to discover what life was like for my ancestors. One story from my grandmother Alda is so remarkable that I wondered if it could be just a legend. However, in the *Chayer Family History*, compiled for the Geist-Chayer Family Reunion in 2000, Roy Chayer wrote words that confirm this evidence of Clement's strength, dedication, and determination:

Clement worked with timber while living in Canada, so he had cut a lot of wood with an axe. Once he and Melina homesteaded near Clyde, Kansas, in either 1874 or 1875, Roy learned from his father that because they had no horses, their farming was done by hand, so Roy's father, John, often saw Clement using a scythe or cradle to cut hay. Roy adds that his Grandpa also worked in Concordia, Kansas 22 miles from home. Amazingly, he walked to Concordia at the beginning of each week, then worked throughout the week and walked back home carrying a 48-lb. sack of flour those 22 miles!

If we ever think our lives are strenuous, this illustration of just one aspect of a pioneer family's life should set us straight.

This photo of the Chayer family was taken in 1890. My great-grandmother Emma is standing behind her father.
Roy Chayer wrote that hunting often included trapping gophers,

rabbits, and several other animals back then. He added the county paid ten cents for gopher scalp, crow heads, and jackrabbit ears!

Another of his contributions shows a difference in the preparation of the foods in their meals. He said his mother cut sweet corn from the cob, put it on a sheet, and placed it on the tin roof of the porch. Once it dried, she placed the corn in a flour sack until it was to be served. Somewhere else in the *St. Joseph Area History*, I read of another wife and mother who scrubbed the ink out of flour sacks once they were emptied so she could make them into dish towels. I'm so thankful for what I've learned about the lives of these settlers in Cloud and Clay Counties, Kansas, from the *St. Joe Area History* booklet and *Chayer Family History*. Even though settlers in your family settled elsewhere, I imagine much of what I've included will mirror what life was like for them.

Another episode provided a glimpse of what it was like to live in a dugout! Mose and Marie Balthazor Tremblay were such a couple. One night, Mrs. Tremblay heard a noise coming from under their table. When she went to find the cause, she found a snake wrapping itself around one of the table legs. Being a brave woman, she killed the snake without panic or upset and returned to bed! Pierre Hebert's activities at a time of celebration took place on New Year's. He had been born in Napierville, Quebec, in 1839. After moving to St. Joe from Bourbonnais, Illinois, he operated a grocery store. It is said that he helped prepare a great deal of food on New Year's Day, including Jell-O in a dishpan, to feed his children who came home for the holidays. The story says that they played the piano, sang, and did lots of visiting and that Pierre loved this merriment. Late in life, he went to the Shrine of St. Beaupre in Quebec to pray for his diabetes to be healed; however, he died at his daughter's home in Kankakee.

The above story reminded me of how families spent their limited leisure time in the days before television and radio. They may not have had Broadway plays or even theaters in small towns of the Old West; but many schools had stages in the front of the schoolroom where the children entertained at Christmas and other seasons with music, skits, and recitations to name a few. The schools were used for other social events, too, making good use of the investment in the building. We're missing out on one type of get-together in this modern world—the box social! Women prepared tasty foods and placed them in decorated boxes. There were no tags indicating whose box was prepared by each woman. The men would then place bids for a box of their choice, supposedly not knowing which was prepared by their own wife. The highest bidder got to not only eat the contents but also enjoy sharing it with the woman who prepared it!

Churches provided wholesome activities too. They had several organizations, as a rule. There were the Men's and Women's Associations as well as groups of people who attended Sunday school classes, the choir, and many other groups who occasionally met to celebrate the seasons of the church year and secular holidays. Another very popular way to socialize, sometimes weekly, was the barn dance and, of course, dances at other locations. My grandmother told me she played a pump organ for dances in her neighborhood on Saturday night and then played for church the next morning! Her mother, Hattie Brockway Girard, made sure her six daughters all took piano lessons, and I imagine some of my great-aunts played for dances too! Other musicians provided music as well—guitars and banjos, I imagine. They must have had a fabulous time!

When telephones entered the scene, they were a great blessing for ordinary uses like business calls and staying in contact with family and friends. However, special ring patterns were developed so citizens could discover what emergency had occurred and how they could help if at all possible. The earliest telephones were crank type. Party lines were still in use in the 1940s, and I'm sharing this because many people born more recently may not have imagined how a thing like your phone number changed through the years. My family's number was 3353W when I was in grade and high school. Why the "W"? A family on the opposite side of town had the number 3353E.

Discovering Heroes That Amaze Me!

The above drawing illustrates a problem that had to be solved as small towns grew. How to get rid of the huge numbers of telephone lines strung from telephone pole to telephone pole! Once electricity reached towns, those who could not afford radios went to the home of a more fortunate family to listen. Radios are reasonable now, so you may wonder why everyone couldn't afford them. One reason may have been their size. I remember my grandparents gathering by a radio in a cabinet the size of a modern-day credenza. I remember begging to stay up late while I was in grade school in order to listen to my favorite program, *One Man's Family*, which came on at 9:15 p.m. On Sunday nights, my parents and I listened together to a lineup of half-hour programs. A mystery program I recall was *The Shadow Knows*.

Humor could be found on variety shows, such as the *Jack Benny Show*. Even great dramas captured our attention, often with the name of the show including the sponsor, like *Lux Radio Theater* and *Hallmark Hall of Fame*. Television arrived in 1952, I think. *The St. Joseph Area History* wrote that Ray Begnoche had one of the first televisions in his St. Joseph Store, and men got home early or stopped by his store to catch a World Series game or a boxing match. The music store next to my father's cafe in Greeley had its first television placed right inside its front window. The first time I watched was during the Republican Convention that selected Dwight Eisenhower. I later saw *Liberace* with a candelabra on the piano and ran home to tell my mother, "We've got to get a TV!"

The St. Joseph Area History mentions children walking or riding horses to school. When I read how some got to school by horse and buggy, I recalled a story Great-aunt Lenora sent me about getting to school during a winter storm. It was so special to me that I wrote this poem about it:

"*The Button*"

It's about my Great Aunt and my dear cousins, too,
I'm thankful she shared what I'm sharing with you.

The hero depicted by my Great Aunt, Lenora was Philip, her father, my great grandfather.

It didn't surprise me, the love she revealed for this Kansas farmer who toiled in his fields,

For my Grandma told me how much she adored this hero to her, and now I know more—

For along with this story my Great Aunt wrote was a button she saved from her Papa's coat

Discovering Heroes That Amaze Me!

And here's the event to which I refer—When the icy wind raged, blowing snow from the North,

It never kept them from venturing forth to the one-room school with the warm, roaring fire

Where local children were taught to aspire to greater achievements than ever before.

Her Papa knew this, and he wanted more, for all his children, six girls and one boy.

Whom, I am sure, brought him endless joy.

One of those morns when the snow drifted high,

He donned coat and cap when he noticed the sky.

Then hitched up two mules to an improvised sled, all while the children were still abed.

Their mother, Hattie, heated bricks and more,

a charcoal foot warmer to place on the floor.

Once the children were tucked in with quilts to stay dry,

O'er fields and through ditches that sled seemed to fly.

And when they arrived, they were greeted with cheers by their teacher and children whose homes were quite near.

And I bet by day's end when the lessons were done they exclaimed to their Papa that school was more fun

When adventure was part of the overall day and

your Papa had taught you what words could not say,

That he cared more deeply than they'd ever known,

By giving them knowledge for when they were grown.

The King's Daughters

It was like a miracle to discover the history of the King's Daughters because there is so little written about many women's lives. When I first saw the picture below, I wondered if I had an ancestor who was actually the daughter of a king! No, they were not the offspring of King Louis XIV but part of a program that provided state patronage, not royal or noble parentage. The King's Daughters were young women for whom King Louis paid one hundred livres to the French East India Company for their crossing, as well as providing a trousseau and a dowry in the hope they would become wives of the Frenchmen already in New France.

Many of the young women were commoners of humble birth between the ages of sixteen and twenty-five. A few came from other European countries, including Germany, England, and Portugal. All chosen were held to high moral standards and had to be judged physically fit in order to survive the hard work demanded of a colonist. I have been notified by MyHeritage.com of more who were ancestors of mine, but these were among the first who I selected because excellent facts were available.

The program could only be described as extremely successful, as judged by the fact that nearly 700 babies were born to the 770 to 850 *filles du roi* who settled in New France between 1663 and 1673. I regard all who participated admirably as *heroic*, including those among my own ancestors. It's sad to discover how rare it is to find out much about our female ancestors, so I'm thankful the history of the King's Daughters has been preserved, as I am sure others with descendants of the King's Daughters who ended up in America are thankful that this history has been preserved. Wikipedia is a good place to start learning about these amazing young ladies. It also provides a large number of references where further facts are available.

Tip: It is fortunate to find both birth and death dates for female ancestors, but don't give up if dates are missing in the first record you find. Try looking at records of other siblings and both parents. If all else fails, I do a Google search with any information that may help bring about a good result. At first, I only searched on key names, places, etc.; but once I phrased my searches in the form of a question or description of what I hoped to learn, my luck increased!

I doubt I would ever have known about the King's Daughters in my ancestry if MyHeritage.com hadn't sent their "matches" about those in my family history. Now I am so thankful I was able to add as much as I could find about them for my descendants and readers who are grateful for this discovery.

Elizabeth Isabelle Doucinet Bedard: This ancestor was baptized on May 19, 1647, at the Calvinist Temple of La Rochelle, France. She was the daughter of Peter Doucinet and Florence Cantau and sister of Marguerite Doucinet, who arrived in New France on August 11, 1666, at the age of nineteen, with two hundred pounds for a dowry. She married Jacques Bedard on October 14, 1666. He was a carpenter, the son of Isaac and Marie Girard Bedard. My first question about this first King's Daughter reported to me was "What was Elizabeth's life like?" When I learned the couple had seventeen children, the answer was clear that her time was largely taken up giving birth to and trying to raise descendants that would survive!

From what I learned of the recipes served at Les Filles du Roy, a restaurant in Montreal, she must have made lots of "Little Bird Pies" as well as "Yellow Pea Soup." I saw the restaurant in a "Generation Projects" episode on the BYU channel and learned of the limited variety of dishes those early settlers were able to prepare because they were limited to what they could grow or hunt in the early days of their new country.

Marguerite Doucinet/Doussinet Matou Labrie: Information I found on Marguerite revealed an important designation of the young women who went from Europe to New France between 1634 and 1663. They were referred to as *filles à marier* (marriageable women) who emigrated based solely on their willingness to marry soon after they arrived. Around 262 filles à marier arrived in New France during that period of twenty-nine years!

Here's what little I know about Marguerite. She was born February 14, 1644, in La Rochelle, Aunis, France, and died on September 15, 1698, in Montreal, Quebec, Canada. She married Philippe Matou Labrie on December 28, 1662. They had ten children, and the only other information I found about this couple was where they lived in 1681, Petite-Riviere-St. Charles-Quebec.

Marguerite Deshaies Ménard dit St. Onge: Another Marguerite, this King's Daughter was born in 1646 in Rouen, Haute Normandie, France. She died on November 17, 1709, in Repentigny, Quebec, Canada. Marguerite's parents were Alexandre DeShayes-St. Cyr and Marie Anne Deshayes Paulet. Her husband, Pierre Menard St. Onge, was born on February 29, 1636, in Vercheres, Quebec, Canada, and died there on August 23, 1688. His parents were Pierre and Madeleine Forest. Marguerite and Pierre had seven children. Thanks to Wikipedia, we know Pierre's occupations were soldier, shoemaker, and notary.

Marie Deshaies Bétourné LaViolette: Born in Rouen, Normandie, France, in 1649, Marie married Adrien Betourne LaViolette between 1668 and 1669. He had been a soldier in the Carignan-Salière Regiment in the company of Captain Berthier. Marie Deshaies must have married at the age of thirteen, since her son was twelve years old when the census of 1681 was taken. In that census, Adrien Bétourné had a gun, two horned animals, and six acres worth of land. The couple had four children. Their story speaks to me of the humble circumstances of many of these early couples who must have sacrificed greatly to populate New France! Marie died on December 18, 1707, in Montreal, Quebec, Canada. Adrien Bétourné died on March 1, 1722, in LaPrairie, Quebec, at the age of eighty-seven years. He was buried the same day in the same place.

Catherine Barre Chaille: One of the first families in the French settlement of Beauport was the Chailles, headed by Catherine Barre and her husband, Mathurin Chaille. Catherine was born about 1644 in the Parish of St. Martin, Ile de Re, La Rochelle, Aunis, France. She was the daughter of Jacques Barre and Francoise Chauvritte. She arrived in the small colony as a filles du roi contracted to marry Maurice Rivet. Upon her arrival, the arrangement was deemed unsuitable, either by Maurice or Catherine herself, and the marriage was annulled on November 17, 1664. Now free to shop around, she instead chose new arrival Mathurin Chaille, and the couple was married on January 11, 1665, in Ville De Quebec. At the time, there were several seigneurs recruiting settlers, and often, they or their agents would simply show up at the docks as an immigrant ship made its arrival, and convince as many as possible to head in their direction. As it was, Beauport was already well established and close to the Quebec Port, so the newlyweds chose that area to build their first home. Soon their son Claude was born; and by the 1666 census, there were four members of the Chaille household, which included an eighteen-year-old servant, Francois Chauvreau.

In 1668, the first seigneur of Beauport, Robert Giffard, died; and his land passed to his son Joseph. Not as easygoing as his father, Joseph went after any tenants who had fallen behind on their lease payments, and on June 18, 1668, eighteen inhabitants of Beauport had their concessions revoked, and though they protested to the Lord's Council, the evictions were upheld. The Chaille family may have been among them, since it was about that time the family could be found further downriver at Sillery. They eventually settled in Portneuf. Catherine died on July 16, 1707, in Ville De Quebec and her husband a week later, on July 23. They had six children; five of whom grew up to raise families of their own. One descendant was my great-grandmother

Emma, whose name was recorded as "Chayer," what it apparently sounded like to the registry officials.

Tip: It is rare to find such a great biography as I found on the Chaille family! I recently learned to translate all the Google searches shown in French in order to find the most information quickly. It opens up the reference in English, which I've learned is not always available within the document.

At first, I thought the story of the filles du roi was just a fascinating event in history, but looking for a photo of "The King's Daughters" restaurant in Montreal, I found an amazing array of organizations that show the spirit of the King's Daughters is alive and well, doing good for the people of today's Quebec. Here are a few illustrations of the many activities that bear their name:

And one more tip, maybe the most important! I earlier searched for a plaque listing the founders of Baie-Saint-Paul, but I didn't note the link and couldn't find it later. I found this memorial plaque to the filles du roi, dedicated in La Rochelle on June 15, 2013, the 350th anniversary of their first departure from LaRochelle. Fortunately, I saved it! So be sure to start "A List of Links" and put important sources in that document!

Artist Ancestors

Tip: Including these artist ancestors is not to glorify my heritage but to include everything I can that may lead to picture collections and lists of interesting facts about those who share ancestors with me. What I desire most is to learn what their lives were like and, as a byproduct, to understand more about history in general. We may all discover ancestors in various fields, but my hope for you is to find more than dates and places but also information that enriches your knowledge about your family and what was happening during their lifetimes!

Clarence Gagnon: There are several instances of marriages between Girards and Gagnons, but hours and hours of searching failed to find this talented ancestor's family unit. Almost all Gagnons in Canada are related, so I felt fine about giving him the most prominent position in my list of artist ancestors, as he is the one whose work I appreciate most.

My curiosity about Gagnon caused me to discover other ancestor artists whose galleries I wish I had known about when I was young enough to travel to Quebec. However, I wrote about it so readers are aware of these treasures to our north!

Joseph Arsene Bouchard and Alda Tremblay Bouchard: Well-known artists, along with their fifteen children, who are listed below:

- Marie-Rosee Bouchard, fiber artist, hooked rugs, painter (1910–1994)
- Marie-Cécile Bouchard, painter (sr.) (1920–1973)
- Edith Bouchard, sculptor, painter (sr.) (1924–2009)
- Laure-Marie Bouchard, sculptor, painter (sr.) (1922–)
- Simone-Marie Bouchard (Mary), fiber artist, hooked rugs, painter (1912–1945)
- Aline Bouchard, sculptor, painter (1934–2002)
- Stanley Bouchard, sculptor (1916–1994)
- Joseph-Arthur Bouchard, sculptor (1928–2010)
- Lucien Bouchard, sculptor (1925–2009)

Like most fathers of large families of his day and age, Joseph had to work hard to keep his family fed and clothed, so he ran a sawmill as well as gardening. In the information on the Bouchard family of Baie-Saint-Paul, I discovered the mother of the above ten artist children had the same given name as my grandmother Alda Girard Shroyer. I can never know for sure, but since the Tremblays were relatives and I know of no other Alda in our ancestry, there's a chance my grandmother was named for Alda Tremblay! Her husband, Joseph-Arsene Bouchard, became recognized as the Father of the Baie-Saint-Paul Bouchard artists! Their eldest son was Stanley Bouchard, who lived from 1916 until 1994. His father taught him to carve when he was a child, and fish became his favorite theme, especially trout. However, he also created religious carvings, birds, animals, and relief carvings of Quebec legends. His works were shown in a number of exhibitions.

Georges-Édouard Tremblay (1902–1967): Like his Bouchard ancestors, he is described as painter/hooked rug and fabric artist, also of Baie-Saint-Paul. He painted landscapes of Charlevoix County, often 18x24x30x40 and even larger. His works were charming, often described as primitive, colorful, and naive.

Marc-Aurele Fortin (1888–1970): He qualifies as one of my ancestors since he is a descendant of Julien Fortin dit Bellefontaine. During his career, he managed to transform landscape painting into a brilliant style. I chose this example because it portrays Montreal during a storm! My grandfather and his parents came from Montreal to the United States.

I saved these two amazing discoveries for the conclusion of this section!

The first discovery that made me want to hop on an airplane to Quebec was reading about the *Train de Charlevoix*. Of course, I had been aware of gorgeous architecture, especially in Quebec City and Montreal; but the discovery of God's great creations throughout Quebec and the whole of Canada still amazes me when the Holy Spirit brings gorgeous images to my mind.

Discovering the train was after I discovered my connection to the lovely town of Baie-Saint-Paul; a website I can't even recall alerted me to the fact that the founders of Baie-Saint-Paul had surnames associated with my Girard ancestors. Since my second great-grandparents came to the United States from Montreal, this scenic railroad trip, which connects Montreal to Baie-Saint-Paul and Quebec City, was a big temptation for me to find a way to travel from the center of the United States to such a lovely part of Canada loaded with beauty and history.

I later realized I was approaching eighty, and my ability to get around and enjoy all the sites is limited. Now I'm content to discover all I can through computer sites and television travel shows. I also realized I know no one in that province of Canada personally, which could be a problem. Through YouTube, I experienced a taste of traveling on this train and hope to repeat the experience.

The founders of Baie-Saint-Paul in Quebec were Pierre-Paul Gagnon, Noël Simard, and Pierre Tremblay. Where is the Simard Memorial? A plaque commemorating these men's passage in the parish has been fixed on the outside wall of the church located to the left of the Sainte Anne Basilica. It reads, "Pierre Simard and his son Noël Simard were known as Lombrette." They arrived in Quebec from France in May 1657 and were given a piece of land within the present-day Sainte-Anne-de-Beaupré (a few kilometers east of Quebec City).

Baie-Saint-Paul is reported to have the most art galleries of any city in Canada! The painting shown here is by Clarence Gagnon and dates to 1915 and is entitled *Misty Day in Winter*. One of the first galleries in Baie-Saint-Paul was *Gallery Clarence Gagnon*, sixty-one, rue St-Jean-Baptiste where hundreds of his works reside that can also be found on the internet.

Many more recent artists bear the surname Gagnon, and I found a site where the paintings of many are displayed. However, my inability to find it again today caused me to include a tip that may seem obvious, but if I failed at this, I decided I should advise others:

Tip: When you have found something you think you may want to include in a project or for your records, either bookmark it or save a link into a document for this purpose. Why? If you are at all like me, you may squeeze your writing time into small segments and fail to realize how much time it takes to find a treasure among the many sites you accessed. *Or* you may decide your first idea hasn't worked out and you need to replace it with new inspiration. Both of these occurrences just happened to me! I started this vignette with a completely different concept but found it dull. Then when I wanted to show some of the more contemporary Gagnon artists, I gave up finding where I saw them after an hour or more.

For those who tackle my challenge of studying your family's history, I want you to understand that more possibilities may open up for you to add to your knowledge and records of ancestors than you can handle at times. Therefore, I am sharing the fact that more early ancestors who founded a town in Quebec (St. Ignatz) came to me more recently. I was able to include their story. However, a genealogy of my great-grandmother Chayer's ancestors came to me so recently that I doubt I will be able to study and include as much about them as I would like. The list of Chaille/Chayer ancestors goes all the way back to the 1400s in France. The fact I may not be able to cover their story adequately in this book reminds me to reiterate that the pursuit of one's ancestry can become a lifelong ambition. So don't be discouraged if your goal is large, as mine is. Take one step at a time, and build the best family history you possibly can.

Discovering Heroes That Amaze Me!

Another Surprising Discovery

Jacques and Antoinette Bernier

I didn't expect to learn that there were more "discoverers" of towns in Quebec among my ancestors, but just recently, I learned of Jacques Bernier dit Jean of Paris (1633–1713). Jacques was the first inhabitant of Cape Saint Ignace and the lord of Fief Saint-Joseph. Bernier was born in Paris, in about 1633 or 1635. He was the son of Yves Bernier and Michelle Trevilet or Treuillet of the parish of Saint-Germain-l'Auxerrois, the second church of the city after Notre Dame and located on the right bank of the Seine, in the heart of the current metropolis. We know Jacques had attended school since he knew how to count and sign. Whether he arrived in New France in 1651 or 1652 has long been debated. The year 1651 seems most likely since on January 17 of that year the king of France, at the request of the Company of the Hundred Associates, appointed Messire de Lauzon governor of New France. The high offices he had occupied in France, services he had rendered in Canada, and the friendship he showed to the Jesuits were indications that the colony would profit from his administration.

The Royal Vessel that brought Jean de Lauzon to Canada anchored in front of Quebec City on the evening of October 13, 1651. Jacques Bernier, aged eighteen, had made the crossing on the same ship. He was married in 1656 in the home of Governor Jean de Lauzon himself, not at the church according to custom. Witnesses were the governor in person and Denis-Joseph Ruette d'Auteuil. These two men came from Paris, where they were members of the parliament of Paris. Jacques being an official there, too, made it easy to hire this man of great human and moral value. Jacques Bernier, however, had to comply with the ordinances and laws of the country. His three years of learning also spoke well for Jacques, a Parisian who had roamed the mazes of parliament and probably the universities of the region. In any event, he married Antoinette Grenier on July 23, 1656, an exemption having been made of all banns for legitimate reasons and causes. Jerome Lalemant, acting parish priest of this parish, solemnly married Jacques Bernier, son of Yves Bernier and Michelle Treuillet, of the parish of Saint-Germain de l'Auxerrois in Paris, and Antoinette Grenier, daughter of Claude and Catherine Grenier, of the parish of Saint-Laurent de Paris, at the home of the governor, in the presence of Messire Jean de Lauzon, governor, and Sieur d'Auteuil. This marriage was the second of eight contracted in 1656.

Jacques Bernier began his family and social activities in a climate of anxiety and apprehension because of the Iroquois constantly warring against the French. On the Isle of Orleans on May 20, 1656, the three hundred Iroquois landed on the island and reduced to ashes the Huron Village, massacring and capturing their enemies. This Huron Village had been established on the Island of Orleans after July 26, 1650. Jacques Bernier's transactions on Île d'Orléans and Cap-Saint-Ignace are recorded in *The Bernier in New France, 1650–1750*, which was published in 1991. It can be assured with certainty that he took possession of his domain in Cap-Saint-Ignace legally on February 5, 1673. The plan of Catalonia in 1703 mentions twelve lands belonging to Jacques Bernier dit Jean de Paris and his sons. The census of 1681 listed Jacques Bernier as forty-six years old, possessing a rifle, eight horned beasts, and ten acres of land. Jacques had proved to be a clever trafficker and a competent real estate broker. By means of his boat, he could make paid transport between Cap-Saint-Ignace, Quebec, and even Montreal. He possessed, according to one author, a general store where each of the inhabitants of the place came to obtain food and material.

Jacques Bernier's house must have been quite large to accommodate about thirty people, as indicated by the fact that when Monseigneur de Laval decided to establish the seigneury of Vincelotte in the parish in 1683, there were twelve families and forty-seven souls who frequented the house of Bernier! Indeed, the ancestor's house served as a chapel and presbytery for liturgical worship at that time too. The parish was canonically erected on October 30, 1678, but the church was built much later. The first mass at Cap-Saint-Ignace was in the house of Jacques Bernier. The many documents left to his descendants and the history of New France give a fairly accurate picture of the character of this brave colonist.

The first to arrive on the Island of Orleans, almost all honest and virtuous craftsmen, came to this country to create a modest ease and live with more tranquility. Some, but very few, belonged to families at ease and distinguished; the others, though poor, were all remarkable for their integrity and piety. Father Charlevoix added, "A great deal of attention was paid to the choice of those who had come to settle in New France; we are living in this part of America, starting a generation of true Christians, among whom reigned the simplicity of the first centuries of the Church, and whose posterity has not yet lost sight of the great examples which their ancestors left them." (*PG Roy: Quebec City*, vol. 1).

The Bernier couple died after fifty-six years of marriage. Antoinette Grenier left first, on February 18, 1713, and Jacques Bernier on the following July 21. Additional historical information on Jacques Bernier and his children can be read in *Les Bernier En Nouvelle-France, 1650–1750*, which was published in 1991. It contains the biographies of all the children of this couple, who are noted founders of New France. However, to talk about the husband without trying to target the qualities and virtues equally brilliant of the wife would be a mistake. I went to a lot of trouble to include histories of other ancestors but missed the significance of including the following about his wife, Antoinette Grenier Bernier, and I'll start with what a Swedish scholar, Pierre Kalm, observed about Canadian women closely in 1749.

He honestly noted the flaws and qualities of other founders. As it happened from a trip to the English colonies, comparisons come naturally under his pen:

> Here, women in general are beautiful; they are well-bred, virtuous, and a carelessness which charms by its very innocence,

and warns in their favor. In fact of domestic economy, they greatly surpass the English of the plantations, which do not hesitate to throw all the burden on their husbands, while they bask all day, sitting, arms crossed. The women of Canada, on the contrary, are hard at work and pain, especially among the people; we always see them in the fields and stables, not resisting any kind of work. When they work inside their house, they always hum, girls especially, some songs, in which the words of love and heart come back often.

One can be certain that Antoinette Grenier did not have the

instruction of her husband. She did not know how to read, write, or sign as specified in a deed of sale from Jacques Bernier to Gabriel Gosselin on April 28, 1674, in front of the notary Becquet. But one does not need instruction to have faith and to love one's neighbor. What is needed is a good education, and Antoinette received it in France. Antoinette Grenier, the sweet mother of eleven children, had a lot of heart and courage, was pious, and adored her children. One illustration of a miracle cure is recorded in history, as follows:

> At the end of the year one thousand six hundred and sixty-two, Antoinette Grenier, wife of Jacques Bernier, a resident of Île d'Orléans, aged thirty-one, was walking along the river with a child in her arms. She was immobilized by both arms without being able to raise them; she remained in that state for a whole day until she was dedicated to St. Anne, promising to visit her in her Little Cap Church. She received perfect healing on the third day that this accident happened to her, which she testified to be true in coming to give thanks in her church. (Signed: Thomas Morel)

Who is this child that Antoinette drops? If it had been Marie-Michelle, born in November 1660, she would have been able to walk alone without her mother holding her. It is undoubtedly the little Charles born in the same year, 1662.

> At the end of one thousand six hundred and sixty-five, Charles Bernier, son of Jacques Bernier, a two-year-old inhabitant of Île d'Orléans, was consecrated to Saint Anne by his father and mother who carried him to his little church in Cape Town, where, after devoting their faith and trust, took off his bandage from the church, and since that time has been perfectly healed without having ever felt any discomfort, which they testified to me to be true. (Signed: Thomas Morel, missionary priest

and canon of the cathedral of Quebec)

Antoinette Grenier married within a fortnight of arriving in New France. There was even an edict by intendant Jean Talon: "When persuasion does not activate during marriages, the steward may impose a penal sanction." Colbert congratulates him in 1671 for ruling that the volunteers would be deprived of the trade and the hunting if they did not marry within a fortnight after the arrival of the girls show ourselves proud, descendants of Jacques Bernier and Antoinette Grenier, to our ancestors. Our grandmother Antoinette, from the height of her bliss, watches over her many grandchildren and intercedes with her friend Sainte Anne for the protection of her offspring, which today covers the entire North American continent.

Let us end this presentation with the following quote: "In the space of 70 years, in the middle of a population composed of soldiers, sailors, travelers, two illegitimate children only! Is this not the best reputation of Sieur de La Honton's nonsense against the fame of the first settlers of Quebec?"

I have included this list that verifies the ancestry between me and the Berniers:

1. Dallas Errnest Shroyer is your father.
2. Alda Mary Shroyer is the mother of Dallas Ernest Shroyer.
3. Philip Charles Girard is the father of Alda Mary Shroyer.
4. Charles Raphael Girard is the father of Philip Charles Girard.
5. Melanie (Marie, Bénonie) Girard is the mother of Charles Raphael Girard.
6. Clement Luc Fortin is the father of Melanie (Marie, Bénonie) Girard.
7. Marie Louise Fortin is the mother of Clement Luc Fortin.
8. Jean Baptiste Bernier is the father of Marie Louise Fortin.
9. Pierre Bernier III is the father of Jean Baptiste Bernier.
10. Antoinette Grenier-Bernier is the mother of Pierre

Bernier III.

The discovery of the second "town" in Quebec has meant so much to me that I decided to include more information on Cap-Saint-Ignace, the proper way to describe the town. I thought it could take a great amount of study to add to my knowledge of St. Ignace. However, this event struck me as the kind of unusual information one would like to know:

There are many events throughout the year in Cap-Saint-Ignace. Not the least is the Feast of Saint-Hubert September 1–3, held in honor of this saint and patron of hunters, complete with a procession and solemn mass to the sound of French horns accompanying the great organ pipes, a meal, clay pigeon shoot, equestrian demonstrations, and other activities related to the hunt.

One historical site in Cap-Saint-Ignace is the Gamache mansion: "Gamache" is among the surnames connected to my ancestors, which made it a joy to find this photo. It is one of the oldest buildings in the municipality, after the old windmill in Vincelotte.

Tip: The Gamache House and the picture below are examples of what you might discover when you can't find data on an ancestor under their name but instead consider all you can find regarding an area! I Googled the name "Cap-Saint-Ignace" to find this amazing photo:

This postcard from 1901 may have helped me spot some of my ancestors had it been the full-sized card; however, it was an unexpected treasure to me because it must be considered rare!

I have accessed many cemetery listings and seldom found any as complete as this one, but with the help of the records in Findagrave.com, you can answer some of the questions you have about your ancestry using the site and the cemetery records.

Cap-Saint-Ignace Cemetery

 Balard—gravsestone of Louis *Balard*: b. abt. 1649, France d. 23 December 1724, Cap-Saint-Ignace, Québec, Canada (Saint-Ignace-de-Loyola)

 Bernier—gravestone of Elisabeth *Bernier*: b. abt. 1668,

Québec Province, Canada (Quebec) d. 4 April 1744, L'Islet, Québec, Canada (L'Islet-sur-Mer)

Bouchard—gravestone of Nicolas *Bouchard*: b. abt. 1637, France d. bef. 16 January 1684, Cap-Saint-Ignace, Québec, Canada (Saint-Ignace-de-Loyola)

Caron—gravestones of Jean-Baptiste *Caron*: b. 13 April 1692, Cap-Saint-Ignace, Québec, Canada (Saint-Ignace-de-Loyola) d. 6 June 1700, L'Islet, Québec, Canada (L'Islet-sur-Mer) (Notre-Dame-de-Bon-Secours); Joseph *Caron*: b. 19 March 1652, Québec, Québec, Canada (Quebec City) d. 6 May 1711, Cap-Saint-Ignace, Québec, Canada (Saint-Ignace-de-Loyola); and Joseph *Caron*: b. 15 November 1686, Cap-Saint-Ignace, Québec, Canada (Saint-Ignace-de-Loyola)

Cloutier: gravestone of Elisabeth-Ursule *Cloutier*: b. 29 July 1660, Château-Richer, Québec, Canada (La Visitation-de-Notre-Dame de Chateau-Richer) d. 23 October 1699, Cap-Saint-Ignace, Québec, Canada (Saint-Ignace-de-Loyola); and gravestone of Louise *Cloutier*: b. 18 August 1676 Château-Richer, Québec, Canada

Fortin: gravestone of Eustache *Fortin*: b. abt. 1658, Québec Province, Canada (Quebec) d. 21 January 1736, Cap-Saint-Ignace, Québec, Canada (Saint-Ignace-de-Loyola)

Gamache: gravestone of Nicolas *Gamache*: b. 17 April 1639, Saint-Illiers-la-Ville Mantois, France d. 30 October 1699, Cap-Saint-Ignace, Québec, Canada

Guimond: gravestone of Claude *Guimond*: b. abt. 1660, Québec, Québec, Canada (Quebec City) d. 14 February 1738, Cap-Saint-Ignace, Québec, Canada (Saint-Ignace-de-Loyola)

Lemieux: gravestone of François *Lemieux*: b. 12 October 1676, Québec Province, Canada (Quebec) d. 10 January 1745, Cap-Saint-Ignace, Québec, Canada (Saint-Ignace-de-Loyola)

Paradis: gravestone of Marie-Anne *Paradis*: b. 6 September 1681, Saint-Pierre-de-l'Île-d'Orléans, Québec, Canada

d. 26 December 1737, Isle-aux-Grues, Québec, Canada (Saint-Antoine)

Roy: gravestone of Anne *Roy*: b. abt. 1653, France d. 12 November 1719, Cap-Saint-Ignace, Québec, Canada (Saint-Ignace-de-Loyola)

(I edited the above list from Greener Pastures to give an example of why I keep looking for good sources of fascinating family information.)

In the midst of writing this book, including the above cemetery list from Greener Pastures caused me to recognize the opportunity this presents to discover more about these early citizens of Cap-Saint-Ignace in Quebec, Canada. I noticed that the first surname, Balard, was one I hadn't run across before! I found several family trees on him. That led me to discover that Louis Balard and his wife, Marguerite Migneron, also appear in WikiTree, where I profile military ancestors. I scanned the list quickly and found a surname I believe to be among my ancestors. It is regarding the grave of Anne Roy, who was born in France in 1653 and died in Cap-Saint-Ignace on November 12, 1719. This created a new mystery for me, which is what the relationship is between Anne and my second great-grandmother Philomene Brin Girard. If I hadn't noticed the name "Roy" above, I may not have ever found out that Antoine Brin's wife was Constante Roy. Antoine Brin is the ancestor who descended from Henry III of Castile, so learning his wife's name just gives me another piece of that mystery, and yet I gained the additional mystery regarding where Constante was born, who her parents were, and where Antoine and Constante are buried.

I was thankful that when I found the glorious art of Marc-Aurele Fortin, MyHeritage.com had already enlightened me on the relationship of my family to Julien Fortin; it said he was a tenth-generation ancestor. Marc-Aurele was several generations removed from Julien, but the fact it is possible to trace the relationships of Julien and his wife Genevieve Gamache encouraged me. More about Marc-Aurele Fortin appears with other fabulous artist ancestors in this book.

Julien was born in 1620 or 1621 in France, one of the early Frenchmen to arrive in New France. One of the descendants of Julien and Genevieve was Melanie Fortin, who married Moisi Girard, my great-grandfather's father. Moisi was born in Baie-Saint-Paul, the town I fell in love with and wish I had visited before I got "too old" for such a momentous visit! One reason the discovery of Julien and Genvieve Fortin is so meaningful to me is learning how important one family could be to a new country, in this case, New France, which we now know as Canada! His mother, Marie Lavie (or La Vye), died when he was only seven years old. Julien's father, also named Julien, was a butcher. His maternal grandfather, Gervais Lavie, was the owner of the famous Cheval-Blanc inn. There Julien heard stories told by Seigneur Giffard about life in New France. Dr. Robert Giffard was also the proprietor of the Seigneurie of Beauport in New France. Giffard returned to France in 1650 to recruit people in Perche to become a part of New France. Julien, then twenty-nine, departed from Dieppe in Normandy and spent three months at sea before arriving in Quebec in the summer of 1650.

The discoveries on the founding of Baie-Saint-Paul and St. Ignace, which are near Montreal where my great-grandfather was born, are the most exciting results of my research on my family. I may never have realized my great-grandpa Philip Girard's parents were born in Baie-Saint-Paul if I had not become interested in genealogy!

In addition to being thankful I can pass extensive family history on to my descendants, it has enriched my own life greatly in countless ways. I hesitate to add that the people covered thus far are only a portion of all the histories I have on record, but I chose to write about the most interesting information so the content would be intriguing to readers. The last section will add more of why I hope readers will want to begin their own adventure in research of family history.

From Great Britain to Connecticut Came the Brockways

Wolston Brockway

Wolston Brockway: I documented Brockways in my line back to 1180, which stunned me! The individual next to that year was Thomas DeBrockwaye, and it only shows that he was born in England. Wolston, the subject of this paragraph, was born in 1638 at Silver Street, St. Giles, without London, England, and died in 1717 at Lyme, Connecticut. His wife was Hannah Briggs, 1643–1687. Again, to have found their actual address amazed me, and I wanted him to appear first on this list to show that he came to the United States! He became such a prominent name in the records of this surname that I wanted to begin with one that would lead me to the Wolston best known in our country.

Wolston Brockway: He was born in 1723 in Branford, Lytchfield, Connecticut, and died in 1810, in Sharon, Lytchfield, Connecticut. His wife was Dorcas Wheadon (1720–1782). This Wolston's father was Samuel born in Lyme, Connecticut (1693–1757).

Tip: The above short list presents an opportunity to mention how many families at various times in history followed a naming pattern of naming a child for your father, just as Samuel named this son for his father, Wolston! The above is also an excellent example of how often we find several spellings of surnames. Dorcas's surname is spelled *Weeden* in her WikiTree profile; and I've seen it spelled *Wheden*, *Wheaton*, as well as *Wheadon* in my own tree.

The Library of Congress document (No. 2020) states that Wolston Brockway's first home in Connecticut was probably on Duck River, south of the present city of Lyme, near Long Island. He gave his land to his children during his life. Perhaps the latest deed was to his daughter, Hannah Wade, giving her certain personal property, to take effect on the death of himself and his wife. He died in November 1717, at which date his son, Richard Brockway, was granted administration of his estate.

It is impossible for me to include every wonderful revelation I have discovered in this document about one of my cherished surnames. I will choose several to describe, but my hope is that those of you readers who research your ancestry find similar documents that divulge remarkable episodes in the lives of your ancestors. Many of the paragraphs below are of military figures since so much family history is found in military records, especially during the American Revolution and Civil War.

In the third generation, *Gideon Brockway* (1723–1784) served in the American Revolution from May 13, 1775, to December 11, 1775. By April 27, the Lexington and Concord Alarms reached as far as Baltimore and by May 11 to Charleston, South Carolina. Connecticut men hurried to Massachusetts and served under their militia organizations who are remembered for this motto: "God who transplanted us here will support us." It is reported that four thousand men performed temporary duty in the Lexington Alarm. At the end of this action, some men were paid and went home while others stayed for different terms. Gideon Brockway's record indicates he stayed until December 11, 1775.

The next significant biography to include is of *Rev. Thomas Brockway*, who lived from 1744 or 1745 to 1807. He graduated from Yale in 1768 and served in what is now known as Columbia, Connecticut, from 1772 until his death in 1807. During that time in his own words, he served through the troubled times of war, when the life of some of our churches, as well as of many of our noble-hearted patriots, was put in jeopardy. He was ready to share with his people in their pecuniary struggles, proposing "to give in fifteen pounds a year till the enemy withdrew, and ten pounds a year till the Continental debt be paid." But this was not enough. As soon as the news of the burning of New London reached this place, "he started off with his long gun and deacons and parishioners to assist in doing battle with the enemy."

Nathaniel Brockway (born on April 5, 1748) married Sylvia Hunter (born on October 27, 1750). They had lived at Dover, Dutchess County, New York, until about 1790 when in Shodack Nathaniel purchased 550 acres of land in the Van Rensselaer Patent, mostly covered with pine for $350! He built a good house on the Boston and Albany Turnpike (seven miles from Albany) and for several years kept a tavern there, even though he was a very strict Methodist! He kept Saturday night as a holy time and provided teaching in his own home at least once every two weeks. Nathaniel died on either September 7, 1838, or September 8, 1836; either way, he lived a long life for that day and age at around ninety!

Ephraim Brockway, a farmer and innkeeper, was baptized on December 28, 1760, in Sharon, Connecticut. He later lived in the town of Amsterdam in what was later named the town of Jacksonport. In 1811 or so, he and his wife, Catherine, gave power of attorney to Jesse to sell land in Montgomery, New York. I wonder if an early ancestor of mine named Jesse Brockway was the one given power of attorney. The final sentence about Ephraim was surprising to me—it says he was remembered especially for his courage in marrying a younger woman when he was over eighty. (I don't often find personal comments like that but am glad it occasionally gives us a better concept of what life was like for our ancestors centuries ago.)

Marcus A. Brockway was born on February 13, 1844. Private Brockway served in Co. F., Fortieth Regiment of the Indiana Infantry, and was present during all the Fortieth Indiana's hard-fought engagements. After the Battle of Stones River, he fought at Murfreesboro, Tennessee, in which the highest number of casualties occurred on both sides, Brockway was listed on the regimental list of wounded. He was honorably discharged from the regiment on December 6, 1864, and died in Boone, Iowa, in 1864.

I've mentioned more than once how difficult it is to find documentation of the accomplishments in the lives of women, so it shouldn't surprise you that I moved forward to this current century and am adding three Brockway women in more recent times:

Connie Brockway was born in Minneapolis, Minnesota. She is a best-selling author who had twice won the Romance Writers of America Rita Award at the time of this writing. She received a double major in art history and English from Macalester College and entered grad school with an eye to acquiring her MFA in creative writing. Soon enough she jettisoned the idea of writing serious literature for what she considered (and still considers) the best gig in the world, writing romance. Connie continues writing best-selling books and has a long list of them on the market.

Lucina Brockway and her family and friends daily lived with the changing moods of Lake Superior and the air of romance and mystery hovering over its shores. The early pioneers respected the beauty and majesty of Lake Superior but feared the power of the lake to brew deadly storms. Lucina and her family treated the Copper Harbor and Eagle River Lighthouses as old friends and witnessed many maritime happenings while living there.

Hattie Brockway (Girard)—I've chosen my great-grandmother Hattie Brockway Girard to represent so many of our female ancestors during the nineteenth century in North America. I only saw her twice (rather, she saw me for the first time as a babe-in-arms, the arms of her husband, Philip Charles Girard, the father of my grandmother Alda I loved so much). The second time we met was when she came to Greeley, Colorado, when my grandfather Walter had died, to be with my grandmother Alda, who was sixty-four at that time; Hattie must have been in her mideighties then. One thing Grandma Alda had told me was that her mother often worked in the fields with Philip, which I would explain as my grandmother having become the little mother to her siblings. Alda and Hattie didn't always have a good relationship. I don't know if Alda and Walter eloped, but I feel it is likely they did, which is why she was so kind and supportive to my husband and me when we eloped.

I asked my close cousin, Jorice, to write more about Hattie, as she was a grandchild of this beloved couple, while I am a great-grandchild. Hattie had been disowned by her father when she married Philip Girard, an older, divorced Catholic from Canada. Jorice added that Hattie feared her father would come after them with a gun and that she would never be able to see her mother again. Hattie and Philip had seven children, and my grandmother told me Philip would take them to "town" (I'm not sure which town) to pick up supplies, and JP (Hattie's father) was often there to see his grandchildren. That seemed disappointing to me, and for that reason, I have often felt sorry for Hattie and understanding of the difficulties in this relationship.

What were Hattie's beliefs? She did not believe in wearing fur or feathers; she believed in women's suffrage and was a Methodist, an officer in the Missionary Society of that church. She quilted weekly with their quilting group, yet she did a man's work on the farm, alongside her husband. Hattie was a "rabid" Republican who read the daily newspaper. I was told that when a representative from the federal government under FDR wanted them to comply with something they opposed, Hattie ran him off the farm!

Grandpa Philip was not able to drive an automobile early in the century, so Hattie took over that job as well. She was a good cook; did beautiful designs on pie pastry; and could also paper the walls in her home, play the piano, and enjoy a good laugh! Hattie made certain that each of her children received a good education and provided music lessons for most of them.

After Grandpa died, Jorice wrote that Hattie visited each of her children before moving to Texas to be near two of them. When Hattie visited California, the family took her to various sites of interest, including the Grand Canyon. Jorice's father felt a little disheartened when nothing ever seemed to impress her. Finally, they took her to the beach to see the Pacific Ocean, and he could hardly wait for her reaction. She looked out across the sea from the shore and said, "I've seen the Republican River (which ran through their farm) when it looked farther across than that!" That causes me to add honesty and outspokenness to the words that describe her.

Discovering Heroes That Amaze Me!

A Challenge to Cope with—My Chayers Who Were Chailles

My grandfather's mother was Emma Chayer Shroyer, but her maiden name was not meant to be Chayer. I read that government officials who registered her family here spelled what they heard, and since the Chailles had come to the United States from Quebec, they didn't speak English. Why this significant error wasn't corrected is a question I can't answer since over 150 years have passed since the birth of my great-grandmother Emma, who was born in 1867. Her father, Clement, was born in 1831, and I have some knowledge about his ancestry back to Mathurin Chaillé, born in 1633 in New Aquitaine, France. He died on January 24, 1687. One wonderful story that I'm thankful came my way is covered in the section on "The King's Daughters" since Mathurin married Catherine Barré, one of those King's Daughters, and settled in Quebec.

Just recently MyHeritage.com sent me detailed data on noted Chailles going back to the 1400s in France. This is wonderful but causes me to admit decisions I made that keep me from adding a great deal to this surname, as well as the surnames of my mother's ancestors. Early efforts showed me that accessing data from countries whose language you don't know enough about can be difficult. Therefore, I chose other surnames with more available backgrounds to include in my records.

Adding some data on those Heindels and Renzelmans will fit in nicely with part 3 of this book. Upon receiving the following list on Chailles, I have to stress that setting limits to how far you will go to cover all aspects of your ancestry early on are advisable. Although I would love to know more about the Chailles and am grateful to have new information on ancestors so far back, I could not have known how time-consuming it is to organize and absorb all the leads that come our way. If I had started my family history study earlier, while my grandfather Walter Shroyer was living, letting him know his early ancestors were so amazing would have been awesome! Here are a few of the early Chailles included on the list: Marie Anne, lady of Béruges and de Bernay *Chaillé* (born before 1470. Her parents were *André*, sire of Béruges, an alderman, mayor in 1462–1463, collector of Poitiers in 1475; and *Jeanne*, dame de Bernay *Rideau* (1452–1538). Her husband was *Joachim*, sire of La Bournalière, lawyer at the Châtelet de Paris, private lieutenant at the seat of the city of Poitiers and mayor of Poitiers. Of course, it is difficult to imagine what life must have been like in distant times; but I'm sure my grandfather Walter, a carpenter who built houses, churches, and businesses, would have shaken his head and said, "Judy, are you sure these were ancestors of mine?"

I expected learning about those early Chailles would be the final surprise in my pursuit of our ancestry. However, a Kansas cousin sent news of another amazing discovery. He received a list which ends with Great-great-grandmother Philomene Brin Girard being included as a descendant of Henry III of Castile! It may be some time before I can go over this data with a fine-tooth comb, but a preliminary check in my tree of over ten thousand people in MyHeritage.com confirmed many connections with several of the surnames listed.

Henry III of Castile (1379–1406)

I have chosen a few of the descendants who gave proof of this relationship to me:

The first was Lt. General Michel Boudreaux, who lived from 1601 to 1688. A daughter of his son Charles was the first I found in which the surname was spelled *Boudreau*: Marie Anne Boudreau (1733–1788)

Antoinne Brin (1811–1850) was the son of her daughter

Marie Suzanne Dupuis (1757–1834)

and Antoinne was the father of

Philomene Brin (1840–1908)

My great-great-grandmother!

Although I don't have enough information on Philomene Brin Girard's ancestors to include in this book, I will hope to gain enough to share with my descendants someday. My feeling is that the most genealogy we can document and share with close relatives can enrich their lives and, in some cases, help with issues of health.

Conclusions and Why Did All of This Matter to Me?

Speaking (or writing) of what you will gain if you decide to take up genealogy, a cousin hinted I try to do too much already, so what did I do? I decided to take on a third project, partly because of a booklet of data I collected on Girard ancestors centuries back. I must have spent a great deal of time up to thirty years ago assembling this handwritten notebook because I estimate there may be hundreds of individuals recorded there. I remember how excited I was the day I discovered Wikipedia had a page on Count Girard I of Paris. What was known about the count, his father the viscount of Limoges, their wives and children was the biggest thrill I could have ever imagined; so, of course, I began absorbing and recording what I could, whether I understood it very well or not! In fact, I'm just beginning to gather enough to understand the lives of the children of Count Girard of Paris I and his wife, Rotrude, granddaughter of Charles Martel. It is important to clarify that whether this data is accepted by all experts is questionable, but I have read enough documents that convince me of who these people were and how they were related to allow me to include them in this book.

A basic gain from gathering facts regarding the ancestors of my grandparents was the assurance of known racial characteristics. Since Antrim is so easily linked to a specific location, I became extremely proud of discovering that my grandfather Walter's grandmother's surname being Irish could account for my love for the importance of music in my life! Until I dug deeply into the history of how my English assigned us that wonderful surname; however, I hated learning that the children of the Irish were taken to England because their parents couldn't pay taxes to the crown! That kept me searching until I discovered the probability that we were previously members of the MacDonnell clan of Scotland. This example alone shows how much genealogical history is not learned through traditional world history, which can stagger the mind! I'll get back to the huge contribution Girard history added to my current understanding of who I am, but, first, I'll continue with my grandfather Walter's family history.

His grandmother Keziah Antrim married Adam Shroyer, a surname

Discovering Heroes That Amaze Me!

I mistakenly thought was French. I got lucky, though, when I began looking for references for Keziah's husband, Adam. I stumbled across an ad in an Illinois newspaper for children of George Washington Shroyer to contact their mother because their father had died and they were named in his will. Then, upon further research, I learned Adam's father, Matthias, had an awesome history I would be sad not to know. He served as a German soldier in the American Revolution in the German Regiment of Pennsylvania. More amazing to me was to learn he developed the muskets which were the guns used in the Revolutionary War!

Little did I know in those early days of my family research that my grandfather Walter Shroyer's mother's genealogy would be even more surprising than other amazing discoveries! I included how MyHeritage.com sent me a family tree including ancestors with the surname Chaille from 1470 to 1672, and I have additional information for periods after that date. *However*, gaining a clear understanding of complex histories like these Chailles caused me to pinpoint how these individuals were related today so I could include more on their lives in this text. It started with Marie *Anne*, lady of Béruges and de Bernay *Chaillé*, marrying *Joachim*, sire of La Bournalière, a lawyer at the Châtelet de Paris (75), and a private lieutenant at the seat of the city of Poitiers and mayor of Poitiers *Tudert*. Their children achieved impressive positions in the French government of their days and ages. My records of Chailles in Quebec mesh well with the parents of Mathurin (1633–1687), who appears in my writing on the King's Daughters, having married Catherine Barré (1637–1707). My family records continue into the twentieth century, covering the Chailles becoming Chayers from the move of my close ancestors from Quebec, Canada, to the United States. Eventually, the Chayers' move to Kansas and Emma Chayer marrying Marion Shroyer and moving to Colorado provided the link to how my parents and I were all three born in Wray, Colorado. That move is the perfect opportunity for me to introduce the most important discovery I would never have realized without this approximately thirty years of studying the lives of my ancestors!

To share with you how important reviewing what you have collected was, my review brought me to the conclusion regarding what was the most important result of all this effort. That conclusion is highlighted in the next paragraph.

When I had gathered and realized all the places where my close ancestors came from, I was stunned to find they came from seven different countries; and if they or their descendants had not arrived in the small town of Wray, Colorado, by the year 1940, I would not be me!

Now what could be more startling than that?

You see, since Walter and Alda Girard Shroyer's move to Wray brought descendants from Canada as well as England, I needed to simply review the fact that Alda's Brockway ancestors beginning with Wolston Brockway, born in 1638 at Silver Street, St. Giles, without London, England, adds England to Canada in the countries of my ancestry. Wolston died in Lyme, Connecticut, in 1717.

Two other countries that fit into this count of countries that are associated with my grandfather are Ireland and Scotland. Both are because his grandmother Keziah descended from Thomas Antrim, who arrived in America on the *James* in 1635. The history of how their proper surname should have been McDonnell is covered in other parts of this book. The poem "Dunkirk Castle" is evidence of the shocking discoveries you may discover when you research ancestors of long ago!

In addition to something as shocking as children being taken from their parents, I was also surprised to discover how little was recorded about our female ancestors. That's why finding the history of the King's Daughters meant so much to me; at least it gave me greater understanding and compassion for how difficult the life of women who settled earliest in a new country such as New France and the United States was when many of our ancestors arrived!

My mother's families of Heindels and Renzelmans brought immigrants from another European country into my heritage! I have found it is harder to add history from the time they came to America from Germany, but part of their story has been covered in previous chapters. The Renzelmans from Northern Germany, i.e., Kirchdorf near Bremen, and the Heindels from Bavaria, mainly the Munich area, contribute to half of my inheritance! So Germany joins France, Ireland, England, and Scotland to make Canada and the United States the final count of seven countries from whence my family came. This calculation helped me feel deep down inside how important it is to know as much as possible about our ancestors!

The next most important plus for me is that the history of places connected with your ancestors' lives at critical times in history becomes more meaningful and fascinating to you! Can you imagine how I felt when MyHeritage.com sent me the fact that Martin Luther and his brother Jacob are distant great-uncles of mine? And that came after I learned Winston Churchill's third great-grandmother was a sister of my fourth great-aunt! I was slightly less awestruck but extremely pleased that more distant ancestors connected by marriage with my Girards were the first settlers and even discoverers of wonderful towns in Quebec! As stated before, I don't know what you will find out about ancestors you research, but I pray you will thank God, as I do, for the pride you feel that you have ventured into the amazing treasure of personal history that I pray will benefit your descendants as well!

The above discoveries were years ago, but the new revelations keep coming, and there are mysteries that may never be solved. But don't let disappointments discourage you; instead, adopt my attitude that learning as much as possible is better than not having tried to know.

Now I'm on to new mysteries. The revelation that my grandmother's grandmother is listed as a descendant of Henry III of Castile has happened so recently that I haven't done enough to track down all the facts I can find. And I want to gather more facts on my Girard ancestors who descended from Charles Martel, but that, too, could take half a lifetime. That's about what I've invested already in this great project, but I'll keep on as long as God grants me further years into my eighties!

I do want to include another *great* advantage for those of us who research our family history. That is how special it is to add cousins to our list of living family members. I work closely with one who works with me profiling military heroes in WikiTree, and both she and her husband turned out to be distant cousins! But several others discovered through WikiTree and MyHeritage.com have added to my cache of connections and encouraged me through the acknowledgment of the ancestry we share. It makes this gigantic world in which we live feel a little smaller and friendlier than we had imagined.

Until the Norman Conquest of Britain, people were known just by a personal (given) name or nickname. However, as populations of towns and cities increased, it became necessary to identify people further. At first, it was enough to identify people with names such as John the Butcher, William the Short, Mary of the Wood, or John Son of Richard, for example. Eventually, many names became corrupted, and the original meaning was no longer clear.

After 1066, the Norman barons introduced surnames into England, and the practice gradually spread. Initially, the identifying names were changed or dropped at will, but eventually, they began to stick and to get passed on. By 1400, most families in England and Lowland Scotland had adopted the use of hereditary surnames. Gradually, the selection of surnames spread throughout the world. Standardized spelling, though, did not really arrive until the nineteenth century, and even now variations occur. Therefore, I hope the rest of this reference will be as helpful to you as I expect it to be to me.

Tip: By all means, start a document in which you record each new surname you have learned about. My list is alphabetical with each new surname typed between surnames already part of the list. When your list has grown beyond a number you even imagined, you'll be thankful you did, as I can't tell you how many times I have accessed my list only to find the name was already there!

When I first became so serious about studying my family history, I only had Familysearch.com and MyHeritage.com to access knowledge beyond the seventy-five or so people I had gathered by questioning my living family members. I don't even know how it happened, but about five years ago, WikiTree asked me to become a trusted genealogist. WikiTree is important for you to know about whether you want to commit to being a trusted genealogist or not because of lists that show everyone profiled with a given surname, but for all of us who do join as a genealogist, we have the satisfaction of contributing to "One Human Tree"—the goal of WikiTree! I would love to be able to write another book on future searches; however, in the meantime, I sincerely hope your family study brings you surprising and fulfilling knowledge and enjoyment!

About the Author

Judy Dimmick is a retired marketing assistant who worked as a church secretary for twenty years, a word processor and a marketing assistant for nearly twenty years for three banking corporations, and a retired marketing assistant for civil engineers in Las Vegas, Nevada. *Dare to Discover* is her first book, though she has written poetry for decades and is currently a WikiTree trusted genealogist, writing profiles for military heroes, her own ancestors, and others. She is also a mother, grandmother, and great-grandmother who lives near Oklahoma City, Oklahoma.

www.ingramcontent.com/pod-product-compliance
Lightning Source LLC
LaVergne TN
LVHW091600060526
838200LV00036B/932